TEDBooks

Who Are You, Really?

The Surprising Puzzle
of Personality

BRIAN R. LITTLE

TED Books
Simon & Schuster
New York London Toronto Sydney New Delhi

TED Books

Simon & Schuster, Inc.
1230 Avenue of the Americas
New York, NY 10020

TED, the TED logo, and TED Books are trademarks of
TED Conferences, LLC.

First TED Books hardcover edition August 2017

TED BOOKS and colophon are registered trademarks of
TED Conferences, LLC.

SIMON & SCHUSTER and colophon are registered trademarks
of Simon & Schuster, Inc.

For information about special discounts for bulk purchases,
please contact Simon & Schuster Special Sales at 1-866-506-1949
or business@simonandschuster.com.

For information on licensing the TED Talk that accompanies
this book, or other content partnerships with TED, please contact
TEDBooks@TED.com.

Interior design by: MGMT.design
Interior illustrations by: Tang Yau Hoong

Manufactured in the United States of America

10 9 8 7 6 5 4 3 2 1

Library of Congress Cataloging-in-Publication Data is available.

ISBN 978-1-5011-1996-5

ISBN 978-1-5011-1997-2 (ebook)

For Hilary and Benjamin

TABLE OF CONTENTS

Who Are You, Really?

Who are you? It's a nosy question, I know, and perhaps even an uncomfortable one. If I asked you that question over a beer at a bar, you'd probably bolt for the door. But once you realized I was merely an inquisitive psychologist, I suspect you'd have a list of personality traits at the ready. "I'm an extravert," you might say proudly. Or "I'm a nurturer," or "I'm a worrier," or "I am the fifth least narcissistic person on earth." Each of us has a sense of the basic traits that define us.

Next, if I asked you *why* you are that way, you'd probably also have some answers already in your quiver. "Because I'm from the west coast," you might say. Or "Because I'm an oldest child," or "Because my dad was a drinker," or "Because the Great Recession hit while I was in high school." You'd have good reason to make those connections. It's clear that outside influences—your home life, the community where you grew up, the political milieu into which you were born—have shaped your life and the way you behave.

And that's it, you might think, it's settled. You are who you are because of your inherent nature coupled with the external forces that have influenced you throughout your life. It isn't really that complex, is it? You've spent enough years getting to know yourself that you should have the picture of your personality put together by now. Right?

You'd better settle in, because our exploration of you is just getting started.

You see, genetics and experiences aren't everything. There is a third force that also determines your personality. And when it comes to this force, our usual assumptions have it backward; it's not *who you are* that explains *what you do*, it's the other way around. That, in fact, is the very idea I'm about to present to you. It is an important new way of looking at personality, and it is what I've spent the better part of a half-century researching and understanding.

Your life and your identity derive from more than just your inborn traits and your circumstances; they are borne of your aspirations and commitments, your dreams and your everyday doings. These defining activities are, in two words, your *personal projects*. Personal projects can range from the seemingly trivial pursuits of particular Thursdays to the overarching quest of your life. They include endeavors small and large, from the intimate to the professional, from the mundane to the existential. They range from "taking out the garbage" to "taking out my political opponent." These personal projects, for better or worse, are shaped in part by both our biological traits and our social contexts. But they transcend each. Because unlike nature and nurture, they are one feature of human life that is not given to us by heredity or society but is generated from within.

You might already be wondering how much your activities could really affect something that seems as stable as your personality and sense of self. The answer is perhaps more than you might imagine. Personal projects are central not only to who you think you are but also to how well you are doing in life—whether you are flourishing or floundering, or like most of us, just muddling through as best you can. Your personal projects, in short, are key to your prospects. Learn to understand them and their impact, and you learn to guide your life in the direction you want it to go.

In these pages we'll look closely at your personality in terms of how your life has gone and how it is going now. But we'll also be concerned with how it might yet go in the future. This is where your personal projects come in: Once you can clearly identify your personal projects and their power, you'll also see the degrees of freedom or spaces for movement that are open to you in determining your own course. My own personal project with this book is to help you see and steer your life—and to do this before kids with scrapes, cats with furballs, or friends who really need to talk right now divert you from plotting your future self.

As I want to make this personal for both of us, let's start with my own account of how I came to study human personality. It was an unusually hot September afternoon in 1965 when I cautiously tapped on the office door of Professor Theodore R. Sarbin. Sarbin was an eminent scholar of psychology at the University of California, Berkeley. I was a second-year graduate student eager to join his research group. The door swung open and a voice intoned loudly, "WHO ARE YOU?" I inferred from Sarbin's stentorian voice and the way he drew out the "o" in "who" that this was more than a desire to know my name. He wanted me to declare my identity! Or what role I was playing, what self I was enacting at that very moment. So I said, in a self-mocking, elevated tone: "A seeker after truth." Sarbin rolled his eyes, snickered, and said, "Oh no, not another one."

A more honest answer to Sarbin's question would have been less grandiose but more complex and interesting. I could have described the personality traits that I'd known were mine since childhood: introverted, curious, and affable. I could have described my roles in relation to other people and the world: a psychology student, a passionate dabbler in piano, and a Kennedy supporter still aching from the assassination. But that was a lot to spurt out in a professor's doorway. Besides, even that would not have contained an entirely accurate picture. Because at that precise moment in my life, I was undergoing a radical change spurred by the extraordinary political events unfolding around me, which I will get to shortly.

But first some context: Psychology at the time was still grappling with whether biological or social forces were more powerful, more consequential, in shaping our personalities—what, back then, we called the nature-nurture debate.

"I am, in essence, my brain, Professor Sarbin," I could have said, aligning myself with the believers in nature, or biological determinism. Indeed, the opportunity to explore the biological basis of behavior was the reason I had chosen to go to Berkeley in the first place. Prior to grad school I had been a research assistant in a neuropsychology laboratory, and when I applied to grad school, I was convinced that what shapes our personalities is primarily genetic and neuropsychological—what I call biogenic influences. I believed that the study of the brain would be the best route to understanding who we *really* are.

Or I could have sworn my allegiance to the nurture camp. I was a short, skinny kid from the west coast of Canada, the son of a whimsical Irish father and a nurturing English mother, and raised in a whimsically nurturing environment. These sociogenic influences aligned with Sarbin's view of what shapes our behavior: He saw individuals as the products of social and cultural forces that provide codes, roles, and scripts for how to live.

At the time, there was also a new twist developing around the nature-nurture debate. An interdisciplinary team of psychologists and anatomists at Berkeley had demonstrated that by enriching the external living environments of rodents, they could directly change the animals' brain structure and biochemistry.[1] Animals reared with social stimulation and complex, exploratory objects in their cages ("friends and toys," as the researchers put it) literally had heavier brains and more complex neural circuitry. This was groundbreaking and controversial stuff, carrying potential implications for improving the quality of life for mice and men (and wolves and women). Yes, biological influences were necessary for a full understanding of behavior, but they were not fixed and immutable; change was possible.

By now, of course, psychology has moved way beyond the old nature-nurture debate of my student days. We now know that these influences are interpenetrating. It is possible to nurture our natures—that was, after all, the lesson we were taught by those little rodents with friends and toys in Berkeley.[2]

But as I would come to understand, these answers to "Who are you?" simply don't provide the best insights for understanding our true natures. What I have been exploring since that fateful knock on Sarbin's door is how our singular, idiosyncratic pursuits—our personal projects—not only rival the biological and social explanations for who we are, but transform the way we think about each of them. These projects are even powerful enough drivers to make us act out of character, redefining our very personalities. I've experienced this myself.

As I hinted earlier, I was in the midst of a fundamental personal transformation when I entered Sarbin's office. I had arrived in Berkeley a year earlier in September 1964, the very week that the Free Speech Movement (FSM) began on campus. The university administration had just banned tables from the area students were using to recruit volunteers for freedom rides in the American South. The policy sparked student demonstrations, sit-ins, and teach-ins. Protestors claimed that the massive, distinguished university—a self-proclaimed multiversity—was in thrall to its Nobel laureates and industrial contracts and had little concern for its students.

The FSM captured my imagination, and its impact was palpable. It was a call to action—to get involved in projects that became deeply personal, even self-defining. Suddenly the introspective psychology student in me, one who would rather sing about revolution than start it, felt driven to speak out to overcome injustice. This was new, and it shook my sense of identity to its roots. What's more, that shift propelled me not only to think and feel new things but to act in new ways. This pursuit that I had chosen was, almost invisibly, reshaping the person I was. Projects like "sitting in" or "going to the demonstration" or "seeking justice" were now commitments—acts of meaning with consequences for the person I was becoming.

Which takes us back to the question I originally asked you—the same one that Sarbin startled me with that sweltering day when I knocked on his door: "Who are you?" Understanding yourself as simply the product of biogenic forces prodding you or sociogenic forces shaping you is unduly limiting. I want to convince you that you are also shaped by the personal projects that draw from both your biology and your culture and can, as we will see, transform both. Such projects may cause you to stretch yourself in new directions, to create a sense of meaning in your life. This new way of thinking about yourself will allow us to ask: Who are you, *really*? And equipped with that self-knowledge, you can then understand how you're doing—and begin actively navigating your future.

1 Scanning Your Personality: The Big Picture

So, how are you doing? Are you happy? Are you accomplishing the things that matter to you? Are you living up to your capabilities? Are you able to love and be loved? Are you physically well? Is there some laughter in your life? If you answer yes to all such questions, we might say that you are *flourishing*. If you answer with an emphatic "No!" or even an eyeball-rolling "Seriously, get real," you might be better described as *floundering*. And in between these extremes, we might find you in the middle, doing reasonably well considering the circumstances.

Biogenic traits deeply influence whether you flourish or flounder. You may be temperamentally predisposed to viewing your life positively and optimistically, even though the objective reality that you confront might be rather bleak. Or despite living in a relatively safe, nurturing, and prosperous environment, you may see your life as half empty, or utterly miserable. The forces of nature and nurture that provide answers to "Who are you?" are also key to answering the question "How are you doing?" The relation between these biogenic and sociogenic influences can be simply graphed as:

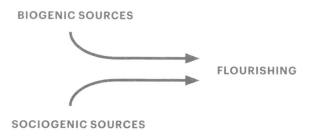

Whether you are flourishing or floundering, in other words, is partly determined by the combination of biogenic and sociogenic sources that impinge on you during the course of your life. These aren't the only influences, but we need to understand how they work before we explore how your personal projects empower you to deliberately design who and how you are. So let us begin with a brief tour through the inner biogenic and the outer sociogenic forces that shape your personality.

Personal Zoom: Scanning the Inner You

Imagine a microscope that dips under your skin and zooms down to reveal your tissues, organelles, cell nuclei, chromosomes, and genes. It darts up to your brain and homes in on a single neuron firing a squirt of neurotransmitters and the explosion of activity in associated cells. It then zooms out to focus on the physical body reading this book wondering about who it is and how it's doing. This "it" is the biogenic you.

Within personality psychology, those who study the biogenic perspective explore how your relatively stable personality traits influence your quality of life. These stable traits correspond to differences in brain structure and function—those microscopic events we just saw when zooming in on the inner you. These biogenic features can be assessed by measures of electrical activity in various regions of your brain or through analyses of patterns of neurotransmitter activity. They can also be revealed through personal genomic analysis, which can now be done for roughly $200. In *My Beautiful Genome*, the Danish science writer Lone Frank relates the fascinating account of her quest to examine aspects of her personal genome and its links to her health and personality. She discovered that she had a gene variant that predisposed her to negative emotionality and what she most agreeably describes as her "own miserably low score on agreeableness."[3]

Some of these biogenic personality traits will incline you toward being happy or healthy or accomplished or, conversely, will explain why you despair over life's various hiccups. Let's say your life is flourishing right now—you are happy, healthy, and successful, certainly compared to your mopey best friend, but maybe even in an absolute sense. This may be due to your having biogenic features of temperament and personality that dispose you to adopt a positive outlook. Even when life sucks, your stable dispositions make you resilient and buoyant. You continue to grow and prosper. Indeed, you may have *pronoia*, the delusional belief that other people are plotting your well-being or saying good things about you behind your back.[4] Your friend's stable traits, in comparison, may not be conducive to flourishing at all. She is angry and defiant and unsatisfied, and according to her mother, she was like this from birth. She is temperamentally disposed to being ill-disposed. She flounders.

The Big Five: The Original You

Did you know that it is virtually impossible for you to lick the outside of your own elbow? And did you know, strange as it may sound, that how you responded to that piece of information—whether and how you attempted the pursuit—might provide a hint about the stable traits you are born with and that form the bedrock of your personality? Let me explain: While there are thousands of ways we might distinguish people on the basis of their traits, personality psychologists have reached a consensus that people vary from one another along five basic dimensions: the Big Five traits. The Big Five have major consequences for how our lives play out.[5] If you would like to get a quick assessment of where you stand on these major traits, the Appendix provides some questions that can guide your own self-assessment.

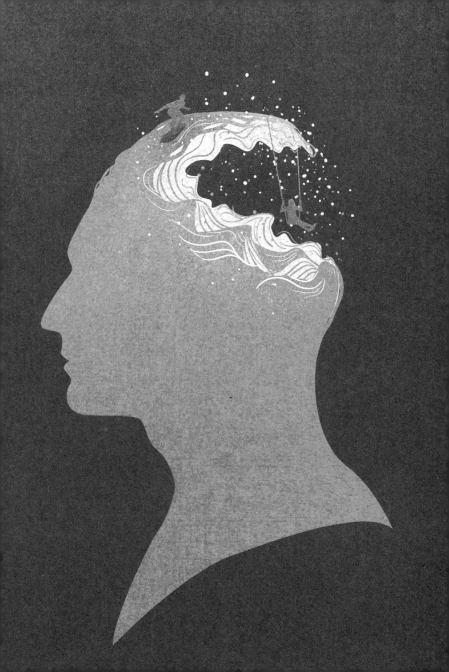

The five dimensions spell out an acronym—OCEAN (or CANOE if you prefer):

Open to Experience (vs. Closed)
Conscientious (vs. Casual)
Extraverted (vs. Introverted)
Agreeable (vs. Disagreeable)
Neurotic (vs. Stable)

Each of these traits has a strong biogenic base, and researchers in personality neuroscience are now identifying the neural structures and pathways underlying them.[6] Because the same dimensions emerge in virtually all countries, cultures, and linguistic groups, these can be regarded as universal dimensions of personality. This doesn't mean that all humans are the same—far from it. Rather, it means that everywhere we go, individuals differ from one another along these dimensions. Also, these five traits do not have rigid boundaries; individuals are aligned with each trait on a spectrum, with most of them piled up in the middle of the range and fewer appearing at the extremes. Here is a short overview of each one.

Open to Experience

Those who are high in openness to experience are easily attracted to new ventures and show alacrity in exploring alternative ways of doing things. Those low in openness prefer the tried and true and would, unlike their more open friends, be very comfortable using a phrase like "tried and true." A landmark study at the Institute of Personality Assessment and Research at Berkeley (now the Institute of Personality and Social Research) revealed that openness to experience was the defining feature of individuals who are exceptionally creative.[7] In an intriguing study by one of the prime developers of the Big Five, open individuals were found to experience aesthetic chills or piloerections—their hair stood up—when exposed to music or art that moved them.[8]

So did you try to lick your elbow? I suspect that if you are game for new experiences, you would have had a go at it. If you are low on openness, you were more likely to just keep reading.

Conscientiousness

Individuals who score high on conscientiousness are particularly likely to satisfy traditional definitions of success. They perform better in academic pursuits and in measures of occupational achievement than those who are low in conscientiousness. It should be noted, though, that these successes are most frequently found in courses and careers that stress conventional problem solving, while those who are high in openness excel at tasks that involve coming up with original ways of doing things. Highly conscientious people are punctual and persevering; they can focus intently on the activities in front of them. This laser focus, however, might work better in some fields than others. For example, Robert and Janice Hogan, pioneers in the study of personality and organizations, devised a study in which jazz musicians rated their fellow musicians on how good they were as performers. Those who scored high in conscientiousness were rated by their peers as *less* effective. Perhaps this is because musicians who intensely concentrate on their playing may be inhibiting the spontaneity crucial to improvisational jazz.[9]

Conscientious adults are likely to avoid drugs, stay clear of dangerous activities, and stick to health and fitness regimens. As such, they are healthier and live longer compared with their less conscientious peers. And the difference in well-being isn't minor: Lack of conscientiousness has been shown to be as important as having heart disease in predicting early death. Conscientious individuals also invest more in work and family roles that reward and increase conscientiousness.

How about their elbows and the implicit invitation to lick them? When I've asked people to do this in groups, the conscientious ones are less likely to lick. Instead, I think they write a note to themselves to check it out when they get home. Those who are exceptionally conscientious, I suspect, will have already googled "licking own elbow" to see if it really is impossible to accomplish.

Extraversion
Extraverts are highly responsive to potential rewards in their environments. They quickly spot and move toward the positive stimulation that they crave in order to accomplish their daily tasks and projects efficiently. This trait, too, has biogenic roots. We've seen the evidence in the fact that extraverts, relative to introverts, perform better on cognitive tasks involving anagrams or short-term memory when their brains are aroused by

chemical stimulants such as caffeine. Conversely, they do worse if they ingest a sedative such as alcohol.

Extraverts' musical preferences turn to the loud, pulsing, and energizing. Partly because of their need for stimulation and their focus on the potential for reward rather than punishment, extraverts are more likely to have brushes with authority like getting traffic tickets or, earlier in their lives, being sent, repeatedly, to their rooms.[10]

One of the most stimulating situations for extraverts is social interaction, and they engage with such encounters readily. Indeed, among the most intensely stimulating social activities are sexual ones—extraverts have been shown to have greater frequency and diversity of sexual experience than more introverted individuals. Introverts can take some comfort, however, in the fact that there is a quality/quantity trade-off in various types of task performance: Extraverts opt for quantity over quality and introverts the reverse. My introverted students tell me these results also apply to their sexual performance. I am open-minded but data-free on this speculation.[11]

When it comes to the question of licking elbows, I strongly suspect that extraverted readers will have attempted to lick their own elbows. They may have also successfully licked the elbow of the person sitting next to them.

Agreeableness
Highly agreeable individuals are particularly effective in groups where they can be relied on to smooth over conflict and build

alliances. Relative to less agreeable people, they are very trust-ing and for this reason might be seen by others as naïve. Highly agreeable people score high on a measure of person-orientation, which is associated with empathy, altruism, and an interaction style that conveys warmth and expressiveness. They also attend to the expressive cues of other individuals, and this contributes to their ability to empathize.[12]

Those scoring low on agreeableness are cynical and dis-trustful of others. They display patterns of hostility that raise their risk for health issues, especially cardiovascular problems. In this respect, they resemble the so-called coronary-prone, or Type A, personality, who is typically time-pressured and hard-driving. It is now recognized that the disagreeableness and hostility underlying Type A behavior is the real risk factor for cardiac problems, rather than their drive to succeed.

How about agreeableness and elbow licking? Highly agree-able people are, well, agreeable, so it is likely that they agreed to play along. Those scoring very low on agreeableness, however, probably weren't game. They may have stopped reading alto-gether and gone outside to yell at their neighbors' kids.

Neuroticism

The term *neuroticism* has a pejorative tone, and though there are some places where neuroticism is frequently valued and sought after (New York City comes to mind), it is generally regarded unfavorably. Those who score high on the neuroti-cism scale of the Big Five are disposed to anxiety, depression, and vulnerability. This does not mean that they are clinically depressed or phobic; they simply experience negative emotions that interfere with their quality of life. Just as extraverts tend to seek out potential rewards when exploring their environments, neurotic individuals are acutely attuned to potential punishment. Not surprisingly, when we look at which of the Big Five traits best predict whether a person will be happy, stable extraverts are the most happy and neurotic introverts the least.

Is there anything positive about neuroticism? In some respects, neurotic individuals are highly sensitive people who, like the canaries in the mine, can detect things that less sensitive people simply don't register—changes in the environment, disturbances in routines, and whiffs of danger from unexpected sources. This is not conducive to relaxed and easy living. But writers and artists and others who are astute observers of life are often found to have a neurotic disposition. In the evolutionary provenance of human personality, I suspect that stable extraverts were the first to discover prey, and we all benefited from eating what they caught. To survive, however, we also needed the neurotic introverts who were especially likely to discover predators. We should be equally grateful to them for decreasing our chances of being sniffed out, hunted down, and eaten.[13]

If you're neurotic, perhaps you have been agonizing over the elbow-licking question for some time and worrying that your ability to rise to small challenges has once again been disproved. But I certainly hope not. Sensitivity is often underrated. And from an evolutionary perspective, we really owe you a lot.

What are the implications here for understanding who you are? There is evidence that there is a genetic base to each of the

Big Five dimensions of personality. These essential traits form our first natures. Yet that does not mean that first natures and the luck of the genetic lottery are the sole determinants of our paths in life.

The Outer Sociogenic You

Now let's take a macroscopic view of you. Imagine a camera zooming out and away from where you are. First, we see an image of you reading this book, then other people in your living room, on the train, or at the café where you are reading come into view. Then we zoom out to catch images of your city, region, country, and eventually the whole earth. These images reveal the complex web of situations, settings, places, and contexts where you and others engage in your daily pursuits.

This imaginary camera has an added feature: It can scan your cyber world, social networks, and virtual spaces—last week's e-mails, yesterday's selfies (even the ones you deleted), and your whole browsing history for the last three years (gulp). And right in the center of this vast interconnected web of social and cultural practices and people is a creature that other people know and call by your name. This is the sociogenic you.

Devotees of the sociogenic perspective explore the situations you confront in your daily life and the larger contexts in which they happen. If biogenic forces shape your first nature, then sociogenic forces sculpt your second nature. From this perspective, who you are and how you are doing do not hinge on your stable traits but on the recurring circumstances of your life. You are molded by the nurturing and opportunities that you're given, the norms you're imbued with, and the ways other people expect you to be. Psychologists adopting this viewpoint wish to understand your roles in life, your social networks, and the prevailing economic and political systems that govern what you do.

For example, in the latest World Health Organization survey of happiness in 156 countries, you might have anticipated that the happiest nations would be those with palm trees, turquoise waters, and drinks with little umbrellas in them. But these are the happiest countries in 2017:

Norway
Denmark
Iceland
Switzerland
Finland
The Netherlands
Canada

Not many palm trees here, although to be fair, the next two on the list are New Zealand and Australia, and they have palm trees galore. But what is common to all of these happiest places is that they are relatively peaceful and prosperous countries. And crucially, they allow sufficient freedom to pursue individual desires and offer support systems like welfare and medical assistance for when things go wrong. If you are fortunate enough to live in one of these countries, your chances of happiness and a bountiful life are favorable. (Of course, the price you pay for flourishing might be freezing your butt off for half the year.)

But Wait: Two Caveats

What if we were to stop here? Is this all you are? What if we concluded that you are a biogenic creature with a brain that shapes you and a sociogenic self with a culture that molds you, and that these forces determine whether you flourish? If we left it at that, we would be making two fundamental mistakes.

First, contemporary research has increasingly revealed that nature and nurture, far from being separate features of the human condition, are intimately linked. Brain plasticity, the capacity to change neural functioning through experience and training, at least temporarily, is now widely acknowledged. Remember those little mammals exploring their enriched cages in Berkeley and gaining brain weight as a result? Those findings, radical and controversial at the time, are now commonplace. Indeed, today there is widespread adoption of programs that are based on the assumption that optimal functioning is malleable. In other words, your social contexts can affect your biology. And the reverse is also true—biogenic personality traits can directly influence the social contexts of your life. Infants who are temperamentally easygoing and affable raise their parents very differently than those who are cranky and tense. Individuals who are naturally disposed to seeking out social stimulation will create very different social contexts for themselves than will those naturally closed to others.

In short, there are vital links between the biogenic and sociogenic factors that shape our lives. So a more accurate depiction of their link with flourishing would be this:

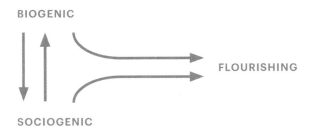

BIOGENIC

FLOURISHING

SOCIOGENIC

Yet there is a second, more fundamental mistake with looking at yourself as simply a biogenic creature or a sociogenic self, even if you assume these identities can interact and influence each other. Both assume that you are a passive recipient of forces that play on you—that you are not an agent of your own development but a pawn moved by the power of genes or environment or both.

The implications of this view are profound. If who you are and what you do are simply mechanical consequences of forces beyond your control, then you lose the capacity for responsible action or for self-change. To think of yourself in this restrictive fashion shortchanges you—it decreases your degree of freedom.

Certainly, it is both enlightening and intriguing to learn about the genetic influences on your personality or the shaping of your life through dominant social institutions. They are necessary for a full account of what it means to be human. But they are not sufficient. To reflect accurately on your essential personality or your options in life or what potential selves you wish to explore, we need a more expansive view of what kind of creature you truly are. We need to change the camera angle.

Third Nature

If we want to understand you fully, we'd start with your first nature, pinpointing your biogenic traits such as where you stand on the Big Five dimension scale. Then we would identify your second nature, the sociogenic influences that supply the roles and scripts through which you engage with your world. But there is a third nature that shapes us in powerful ways. This is your *idiogenic* self, derived from the Greek *idio-*, meaning personal or particular to oneself.

To see the origins of this idea, we need to zoom back in my own history, to a serendipitous encounter with a book that

changed not just my work but my understanding of who I am—
and who you are.

Personal Constructs: Your Goggles for Viewing the World

A month or so before heading off to graduate school, I was
searching my college library for a book on brain anatomy. As I
reached up to where that book should have been, I pulled down
a misshelved tome by George A. Kelly titled *The Psychology of
Personal Constructs*. I had heard some favorable things about
Kelly in one of my classes, so I thought I should skim a few
pages. Several hours later, completely engrossed and aching
from having squatted so long on the library floor, I had one of
those epiphanies that make life so interesting. Although I still
wanted to study neuropsychology, it would have to wait until I
could explore Kelly's theory of personality in real depth.

The essential idea behind personal construct theory is this:
All individuals are essentially scientists erecting and testing
hypotheses about the world and revising them in the light of
their experience. Those hypotheses are called *personal constructs*, and they are the conceptual goggles through which we
view the world.[14]

The critical word here is *personal*. These constructs are in-
dividually significant to you and expressed in your own words.
Constructs are typically communicated as short phrases that
compare and contrast different people, objects, or events. For
example, you may size up other people as nice versus mean,
blunt versus nuanced, bright versus stupid, or high energy

versus low energy. These ways of construing individuals mean a lot to you and have enabled you to negotiate most of your daily encounters. At the same time, your coworker or neighbor are probably working with their own set of go-to descriptors.

Kelly's theory was considered radical when he published his work in the mid-twentieth century. The prevailing views of personality at the time were grounded in psychoanalysis and behaviorism, each of which, taking different tacks, regarded humans as passive creatures. But Kelly's prototypical human—you, for example—is not driven by unconscious biogenic forces or buffeted about by sociogenic reinforcements. You are inquisitive, prospective, and exploratory. And to understand you, we need to know the personal constructs through which you interpret objects, events, other people, and yourself.

One of the interesting things about personal constructs is that they're always in flux. The goggles through which you viewed life in April may no longer be helpful to you in May. As a lay scientist you revise your predictions about the world, you test new ideas, and in the process, consolidate a new set of personal constructs that works for you. You are driven by your own explorations, your active attempts to make sense of everything around you. These attempts are idiosyncratic, singular, and deeply personal. They are idiogenic.

So if I want to understand you, I need to put on your goggles and see the world through your personal constructs. If I wish to understand your personality and whether you feel your life is going well, I need to look at your world through the lenses that you have created. How are you flourishing or floundering in those aspects of your life that are *personally significant* to you?

The implications of this perspective fascinated me. I saw it clearly: To best understand human personality and our capacity to flourish, we need to explore not two but *three* sources of self: the biogenic, the sociogenic, and the idiogenic. The interplay among them can be graphed like this:

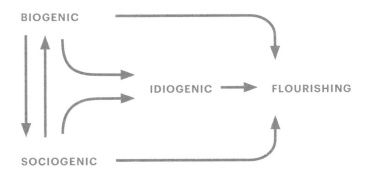

Another Epiphany: On the Road

Two years after stumbling across Kelly's book, I had an opportunity to dig deeper into personal construct theory. As luck would have it, Kelly came out to the West Coast to teach a course on personality psychology at Stanford. I eagerly signed up, and each day drove the fifty-six minutes along El Camino Real from Berkeley to Palo Alto, ready to have my personal constructs challenged. The assignment that Kelly set each of us was not for the faint of heart: create a new theory of personality.

After the very first lecture, I knocked cautiously on Kelly's office door. He didn't answer with a "WHO *ARE* YOU?" but I told him anyway. I said that I believed in the precepts of personal construct theory but wanted to challenge him on two different issues. First, jazz: I raised the question of whether there was room in his theory for *passive* pleasures such as listening to music. Kelly's eyes lit up and he began to talk animatedly about *playing* jazz—how what we identify as a jazz musician's distinctive style is an interpretation of music through their personal constructs. He didn't pick up on my question about *listening* to jazz rather than playing it, but his answer intrigued me nonetheless. I pressed on with a second issue. I told Kelly about my experience with the Free Speech Movement, which I saw as an affirmation of his model of human beings as active determinants of their lives. But I worried that by using personal constructs as ways of studying the person, we weren't paying sufficient attention to the contexts of our lives—the situations, the institutions, the political climate of the moment. Kelly encouraged me to explore it further, and I left his office buzzing with excitement.

On the road back to Berkeley that night, I plotted out some possibilities for a revised theory of personality. I was just north of South San Francisco when it occurred to me that the drive itself, the journey I was on, was more than just the elaboration of my personal constructs. Something was missing. I pulled off the highway, too distracted by the idea taking form to keep driving.

What I realized there and then was that what I was pursuing at that moment was a personal *project*. I began to consider the implications of humans pursuing personal projects in their lives— everyday pursuits that are trivial or transformative, singular or communal, brief encounters or enduring commitments. The concept of personal projects allowed me to bring together both the inner maps that personal constructs provide and the outer ecology of possibilities, like the off-ramps, cul-de-sacs, and open highways that formed the route I was taking.

Your relatively fixed traits set some limits on the destinations that your projects might explore. Your social and cultural environments will open up some paths and shut down others. And the way you construe the journey—the way you define, describe, and judge your own projects—will be central to whether you keep exploring, turn back or, alas, crash and burn. In short, project quests involve the interplay of all three aspects of our personality—the biogenic, sociogenic, and idiogenic—and their success is essential for flourishing.[15]

2 Personal Projects: The Doings of Personality

There are two ways in which you can think about your personality. The first is in terms of the personality attributes you *have*—like the traits of neuroticism, extraversion, or conscientiousness. The second is in terms of what you are *doing*—your personal projects: "get over my social anxiety," "deliver an awesome pitch in my sales meeting," or "stop procrastinating." The study of personal projects, the "doings" of daily lives, provides us with a different perspective and greater scope to reflect on our lives than the study of our "havings" alone. [16]

By now you've caught a glimpse of that most counterintuitive argument with which we began: that what you do affects who you are. This is because personal projects are all about the future—they point us forward, guiding us along routes that might be short and jerky or long and smooth. By tracing their route, we can map the most intimate of terrains: ourselves. Most thrilling is that we can learn to adjust our trajectories, riding over the rough patches and extending the smooth stretches to make our endeavors more effective. In this way, projects help define us—they shape our capacity for a flourishing life. Because in an important sense, as go your projects, so goes your life. [17]

An important clarification: Personal projects are not limited to formal projects that are required of us, such as getting Mom into a good nursing home, although sometimes we pursue them out of a sense of duty. They are also, crucially, acts we gladly choose. Toddlers are pursuing projects when they toddle, and so are lovers when they love. I am certain that our cat has a project when she stalks, pounces, and sits atop our other cat, purring.

Personal projects can also be fairly trivial pursuits, like taking the dog (or the cat that thinks it's a dog)[18] for a walk. But they can also represent the highest reaches of human aspiration and acts of courage. When Rosa Parks chose not to move to the back of the bus, it was a small but courageous act with big consequences. The care you take in getting Mom into the nursing home is more than duty, as it breaks your heart to see what Alzheimer's has taken from her.

Personal projects are extended sets of personally salient action in context. Let's parse this definition. *Personal*: Personal projects are framed through the idiosyncratic lens of the project pursuer. We can't simply watch you build a tree house, or train for a marathon, and surmise what the pursuit of your personal project says about you. In order to truly understand, we need to ask you the question crucial to revealing your idiogenic nature: What do you *think* you're doing? In other words, what does this mean to you? The answer is often surprising.

Somebody observing you right now might infer that you are reading a book. But you know better. You are barely registering the words in front of you because your personal project is actually "appearing to be independent and self-confident so no one will ask why I am alone on this cruise ship." Your reading

behavior is actually a decoy that helps you cope with your rapidly changing answer to the questions "Who are you?" (a recovering romantic) and "How are you doing?" (not bad considering the breakup).

Let's continue unpacking our definition. *Extended*: A project is not a momentary act but typically a sequence of actions that are extended in space and time (from seconds to decades). In contrast with the stable traits that are freeze-frame shots of your personality, personal projects are moving pictures; their full meaning is not apparent until the entire sequence comes into view.

Set: A project encompasses a series of actions that are considered interrelated by the project pursuer. Let's say you are not actually reading this book to hide from your cruise companions, but rather to glean lessons that will help in your pursuit of making new friends on the boat. Besides reading this book, you might read other books, take personality quizzes, seek advice from people who know you well, and join in on the ship's game night. But the woman in a floppy hat sitting in the lounge chair beside you could never know, just by observing you reading a book, what personal meaning it has for you.

Switch this around for a minute and think of how you see others. You might observe the actions of another person who shows up whenever you go to a certain bar, shares the same dentist as you, and is often seen outside your house. Depending on the person who is engaged in that set of actions, their personal project may be "being a partner to my wife," "flirting with my neighbor," or "stalking." Sets of action may be innocent and compassionate. They may also be contemptible. It depends on the project underlying them.

Personally salient: By salient I mean that a person identifies a course of action as standing out from all the other possibilities that might be pursued. A personal project enacts one possibility among all those dizzying alternative possibilities. It is deliberate. And that is because it means something particular to you, the pursuer.

Action: A project is not a passive response to external forces but an intentional sequence of behavior. A blink is not an action if it occurs as a reflexive response to a puff of air. But a wink is an action that has consequences. Notice how subtle the difference is between action and nonaction: Even a blink can be an action if it is performed by an optometrist showing you what to do after receiving eye drops.

In context: Personal projects are enacted in physical, social, cultural, and temporal contexts, and these contexts, as we've discovered, can stimulate, potentiate, inhibit, or block project pursuit.

Personal Projects: A Deeper Dive

Take a look at your own personal projects. For about ten minutes, list the various personal projects you are pursuing at present. Don't agonize over what to write down. At any one time, we usually have a mixture of trivial pursuits and magnificent obsessions. People usually list around fifteen projects in ten minutes, but when we remove time constraints we have seen lists ranging from one project to hundreds.[19]

The content of your personal projects can be very revealing. The first time I administered this type of assessment, which I call Personal Projects Analysis (PPA), to university students, these were the first two personal projects generated by a male student: "Clarify my philosophical beliefs," and "Get laid."

Both the lofty and the lusty pursuits of this undergraduate seemed to capture a certain reality of students' academic and social lives at the time.

We have now studied the personal projects of thousands of individuals and have identified several major types of content. Here are the most frequent types of projects that adults engage in (with the most frequent first), together with some examples:

Occupational/Work: Make sure department budget is done.
Interpersonal: Have dinner with the woman in the floppy hat.
Maintenance: Get more bloody ink cartridges.
Recreational: Take cruising holiday.
Health/Body: Lose fifteen pounds.
Intrapersonal: Try to deal with my sadness.

Sometimes the mere listing of a person's projects gives a hint of a life story unfolding. You may have detected one in the list above. A splendid example of this is a short story in *The Guardian* by Jennifer Egan.[20] It is simply called "To Do," and the first few entries are:

1. Mow lawn
2. Get rid of that fucking hose
3. Wash windows
4. Spay cat
5. Dye hair
6. Do tarot cards
7. Pick up kids
8. Drop off kids at Mom's
9. Buy wig
10. See if small removable portion of fence can be cut QUIETLY . . .
11. Send warning letter
    a. Newspaper cutouts?
    b. Get kids to write it?
    c. Write with left hand?
    d. Be vague. "Certain unpleasant things"
12. Mail letter
    a. Or drop it off while wearing wig
13. Renew meds

The project "to-do" list continues in this fashion and is strikingly evocative, blending everyday parental pursuits with deadly pursuits, underscoring how one's projects can speak volumes about one's personality.

Self Projects

Although they are comparatively infrequent in project lists, those we call *intra*personal projects are especially interesting and important. They are projects focused on the self, such as "try to be less socially anxious," or "become a better listener." Are these sorts of endeavors good or bad for us? The answer is complicated.

On the downside, such projects are known to be linked with feelings of depression and vulnerability.[21] If you have projects of this sort, you may find that you get into a kind of ruminative loop where you can't make progress. You overthink the change you feel you need to make and over-scrutinize your (lack of) progress. On the upside, however, we also have evidence that engaging in intrapersonal projects can be associated with aspects of creativity and openness to experience.[22] Why, on the one hand, is an intrapersonal project associated with negative emotions and vulnerability, and on the other, is seen as a creative adventure? It is likely due to the *origin* of the self-focused project.

Did you include a self-change project on your list? Who told you to listen better, or to get on top of your social anxiety? Who told you to get your values straightened out, you degenerate, before you find yourself sucked into a destructive lifestyle that you can't escape? If it is a parent, boss, or lover who generates the project, it is more likely to create negative emotions than if you yourself were the initiator. There is now a significant body of research demonstrating that "intrinsically regulated" project pursuit will be more successful and lead to greater well-being than "externally regulated" pursuit.[23] If you included self projects on your list, then ask yourself who instigated it? If they spring from your own vision of a possible self, you are likely to feel better while pursuing them. And those projects are ultimately more likely to succeed. Those initiated by others might be willingly undertaken. But if they are forced or coerced, they may be nonstarters.

"Trying" Projects

How else can you improve your project experience and your odds of eventual success? Even the way in which you *phrase* your personal projects has implications for how successful they will be. Some people engage in ambivalently framed projects like "try to be more sensitive to my idiotic coworkers" or "maybe apologize to my sister for calling her boyfriend creepy." Canadian psychologist Neil Chambers has shown that such "trying" individuals are less likely to accomplish their projects than those who phrase their pursuits more directly.[24] Were the projects to be rephrased as "*be* more sensitive" and simply "apologize," they would be more likely to benefit your idiotic coworkers and your sister (not to mention yourself).

How's It Going? Appraisals of Personal Projects

How you think your projects are going is critical to your well-being. Think about it: We all know people who seem to have everything going for them but reflect on their lives as being disappointing. So while knowing the content of your projects is important, knowing how you appraise them is even more critical.

When you take the Personal Projects Analysis, the second thing we ask you to do is to select ten of your personal projects that you think are important for understanding you at this point in your life. You then rate each project (from 0 to 10) on approximately twenty dimensions such as how stressful, how enjoyable, how much under your control, and how visible to other people each one is for you. Over many studies, we have found that these detailed measures can be grouped into five broad clusters: project meaning, manageability, connection, positive feelings, and negative feelings.

Meaning: Personal projects may range from being deeply meaningful to utterly alienating. A sense of project meaning rests on how important the project is to you—how consistent with your core values it is and how self-expressive it is (that it really feels like you).

Manageability: Our projects can range from being well organized and managed to being a chaotic disaster. Greater manageability occurs when you initiate the project, and when you have a high degree of control over it and sufficient time to work on it. The most important aspect of manageability, however, is your sense of efficacy—the expectation that your projects are going to be successful. In fact, of all the different ways of thinking about personal projects, efficacy best predicts whether a person feels that their life overall is going well.[25]

Meaning-Manageability Trade-off: Often we end up

sacrificing meaningful personal projects for manageable ones. For example, the projects that most align with our core values are often quite abstract, such as "be sensitive to the environment," "be more in touch with my spiritual side," or "treasure my family." But because these are not necessarily anchored in the concrete realities of daily life, they may end up drifting and being ignored. On the flip side, you might have projects that you initiated, that are tightly scheduled, and totally under your control but quite meaningless. Every Thursday, you have that lunch meeting with your coworkers, including the idiotic ones. But while you smile away with them, inside you can't stand to hear one more round of weather complaints, sports scores, or kid stories.

Connection and Support: Perhaps you have figured out this meaning/manageability trade-off, and you've set your sights on a project that is both meaningful *and* manageable—say, replanting the yard with native species. Great! But there's another key factor that determines whether this project ultimately builds you up or wears you down: How much support you have from those with whom you are connected. Does your spouse think the replanting is a great idea, or does he or she like the mango trees in the yard the way they are and consider the endeavor a waste of time and money? Fat chance it's going to bring the delight you thought it would when the job ends up being solitary, when you hoped it might be shared and supported by your mango-loving significant other.

Hyperconnected Projects: If you rated some of the projects that matter to you as low on "visibility to others" and not much valued by other people, these are flags that such projects might run into trouble. But you may have the opposite problem—you may be hyperconnected with others. Other people usually initiate your projects, they value them deeply, and you love to share the details of how they're going with them. The painfully detailed highlights of your morning ablutions are visible to them through your *very* social media, where you tweet, Instagram, Facebook, and Snapchat about your deeply connected life.

The vulnerability here is subtler. Your personal projects may be *insufficiently* personal. The direction and meaning in your life derives primarily from others. In many ways, this is admirable, and in some cultures it is expected and rewarded. But when those friends are gone, the kids are grown, or spouses split, there is no center of gravity—no you—in your life. And this can be perplexing.

The Emotional Tenor of Personal Projects: Your life may be imbued with projects that are meaningful, manageable, and effectively connected with others, and yet problems might arise with the kinds of feelings you experience when you are pursuing them. We assess emotion in PPA by asking the following questions: What are the negative emotions you experience? Are your personal projects stressful and frustrating, and do they generate feelings of anger, sadness, and hopelessness? Or are your projects enjoyable and delightful and while pursuing them do you feel love and joy? It is possible that you might experience both positive and negative emotions in the same project, especially in long-term commitments. Highly creative individuals probably know this ambivalence well: It can be deeply frustrating to work on the same music score for three years, and deeply satisfying to release it into the world.

Generally speaking, to the extent that a person is engaged in projects that are meaningful, manageable, and connected with others, and that generate more positive than negative feelings, their well-being will be enhanced. And it is hardly surprising to find that those whose projects are meaningless, chaotic, isolating, and overwhelmingly negative do not flourish.

The Role of Traits in Personal Projects

The greatest value in thinking of personality as "doing projects" rather than "having traits" is in three powerful words: *potential for change*. We can consciously choose and adapt our projects in ways that we cannot change our traits.

But that doesn't mean we can leave our traits back on shore, speeding freely across the water toward a self shaped by projects alone. Our projects and traits are connected. Our research shows that where you stand on the Big Five trait dimensions affects your appraisal of your personal projects—the "How's it going?" part. This has practical implications for which projects you undertake and how challenging they are for you.[26]

For instance, neurotic people have a generalized sense of negative emotions and so are much more likely to appraise all their projects, whether they are interpersonal or academic or work-related, as stressful. If this describes you, there is one practical implication you should know. Make a space in your life for projects that you find uplifting. These needn't be major projects; indeed, it is better if you have frequent engagement with smaller-scale projects that give you a sense of pleasure. Your natural tendency to see the downside of the larger endeavors of life can be offset by frequent, intense experience with the little things.

A more surprising link is between conscientiousness and how we see our projects. As you might expect, those high in conscientiousness rate their academic and work projects more positively, and see these projects as meaningful and efficacious: they get things done and feel good about getting things done. If you are conscientious, you have a trick that helps make you efficacious and positive—you can spin mundane tasks into enjoyable ones. For example, a numbingly boring task can be made more interesting by transforming it into a game where you pit yourself against an imagined opposition or even your previous self of yesterday. Even if you are not so conscientious, this strategy can help you get through a long to-do list.

But conscientious people also see their *interpersonal* projects positively. I have to say that that initially surprised me. I didn't expect conscientious people to be so positive about their interactions with others, perhaps because I held a false stereotype about them as being, yes, highly committed and earnest, but also, at times, rather joyless drudges. That stereotype is just plain wrong.

Extraverted and agreeable people also tend to have positive feelings about their personal projects, but these feelings are especially strong in interpersonal projects. Although both extraverted and agreeable people are sociable, they differ in the kinds of social projects they enjoy. If you are an extravert, you feel most efficacious and positive when engaged with others in exciting social events like parties, even when they may involve the occasional conflict. If you are agreeable, but not especially extraverted, you see interpersonal project success somewhat differently. You enjoy sociable activities, although not raucous ones. And unlike your extraverted friends and especially your disagreeable ones, you really don't like conflict-laden social encounters. In contrast, disagreeable individuals have actually been reported to experience positive emotions when they are doing disagreeable things, such as disciplining another person.

People who are open to experience are more likely to initiate their own projects rather than have them imposed by others. This is consistent with what we know about their capacity for active engagement with the world. Also, those who are more open are likely to choose projects that accord with their core values, in contrast to those who are more closed.

Recent research has shown an important link between traits, personal projects, and well-being. We have already seen how personality traits are a strong predictor of happiness, with stable extraverts being especially likely to be happy. However, the impact of traits on well-being is not always direct. The direct influence is through the kinds of personal projects individuals pursue.[27] For example, a disagreeable introvert is not necessarily constrained to a life of unhappiness. She might engage passionately in writing a politically charged blog. It brings her deep pleasure both because of its intrinsic meaning but also because she loves making others squirm. In short, when it comes to well-being, projects can trump traits. This should give you some hope that you are not the victim of the traits with which you entered this world. Your deeds speak louder than your dispositions.

Acting Out of Character

Let's say, however, that what you wish to do goes against your natural grain. Maybe you are a biogenically agreeable sort, averse to conflict in any form, who nonetheless loves mysteries and dreams of being a hard-boiled detective. Or you're a natural introvert with a chance to work as a sales representative, a job that requires you to be an over-the-top extravert. Or a highly conscientious, regimented planner who wants to become more improvisational to connect with your free-spirited child. Are your dreams doomed? Are you confined only to projects that suit your inborn traits? Not necessarily. Our ways are not as stuck as they might seem. In fact, one of the things that makes you so intriguing is your ability to sometimes act "out of character."

This capacity for shape-shifting is a startling and fascinating aspect of our personalities. Your ability to act beyond the bounds of your personality is where the purpose of my impertinent questioning at the bar becomes fully clear, because the reason we often take on new traits is to more effectively pursue our personal projects. This is how *what you do* can remake *who you are*—and it's a revelation that turns previous ideas about human personality on their heads.

How exactly does this work? Well, it is a fact of living that we sometimes want things that require us to stretch ourselves to achieve them. So an agreeable person may act disagreeably to book an urgent appointment with an in-demand physician, or a biogenically anxious person may appear poised and unruffled when first meeting her in-laws. These people are engaged in what I call "free traits." And they are doing so to more successfully pursue a personal project.

You typically enact free traits with the best of motives, but they may "trick" others into thinking that you are, say, agreeable when in fact you are a biogenically disagreeable person. Or stable when you are highly neurotic. Or extremely extraverted except that you overload easily, are sleepless after caffeine, and prefer to curl up with a below-average book than go seriously crazy at the Boom Boom Room. So when we meet and I begin to form my impressions of you, is what I see displayed who you are, *really*? Is your behavior a trick or a trait? Perhaps neither. It could be a *free trait*.

For example, many are surprised to find out that Robin Williams, the late comedian and actor, was a self-professed introvert. In a fascinating interview, James Lipton, the host of *Inside the Actors Studio*, tells Williams that Mike Myers, also a comedic actor, had described himself as being a *site-specific extravert* but an introvert most of the time. Williams affirmed that he was the same, describing himself as "introverted, quiet, and absorbent."[28]

The notion of site-specific extraversion is essentially what I mean by the enactment of a free-trait behavior. With Myers and Williams, the extraverted behavior is *literally* scripted, part of the role they are playing to advance their personal projects of being successful actors. But many of us also engage in such behavior; our scripts may be metaphorical, but they similarly ask us to act in ways that go against our biogenic dispositions.[29]

Consider having a job as a flight attendant or a debt collector. Each has an associated personal style that may or may not align with the biogenic personalities of those who work those jobs. A grumpy, taciturn, impatient flight attendant isn't going to last, nor is a sweet, engaging, and forgiving bill collector. But a person who is not biogenically suited to a certain role may still desire to fill it. So to survive in their fields, they become *site-specific free-trait adopters*. At first this can be difficult, but during the course of developing their occupations, they practice again and again until it becomes more natural. Though seasoned travelers might be able to spot them, pseudo-hospitable flight attendants are generally able to pass. Their professional roles matter to them.[30]

Or consider the case of Victoria. She is a genial and generous person who is agreeable to a fault. But she has been trying to get her mother into a care facility for six months with no success. She loves her mom dearly and sees her cognitive decline progressing rapidly. But Victoria is stonewalled at every turn by bureaucratic intransigence and bored indifference. So she adopts a free trait and becomes a site-specific pain in the ass. Hurricane Vicky is most definitely not a pleasant person at the care facility, but her mom is admitted and that personal project of hers is a success.

If we practice such free traits often enough, they can creep into our personalities in more pervasive and permanent ways. "I pretended to be somebody I wanted to be and I finally became that person. Or he became me. Or we met at some point." This quote, by Archibald Leach, perfectly demonstrates the power of using free traits to shape who you are. Archibald was a high school dropout, a traveling circus performer. But he wanted more, a bigger life. When he began to gain success as an actor, he changed his name to the one we all know him by: Cary Grant. By consistently acting the part of the cool, confident, witty charmer he eventually, as he put it, truly became that person. Or that person became him. And he flourished.

The phrase "acting out of character" actually has two meanings. It means acting *away* from our characteristic way of behaving. But it also means acting *from* character. We often act out of character in the second sense when we guide our actions by our values. You may not be naturally open and extraverted. But given an important occasion or project you have little choice but to act out of character, to rise to the occasion and be an alternative you—in a sense, perhaps, an optimized you.

Restorative Niches and Burnout Prevention

Acting out of character—and against one's first nature—can be psychologically and physiologically depleting. So how do we recharge after the stressful effects of free-trait behavior? By finding or creating the right environment, or what I call a *restorative niche*, to reconnect with our biogenic selves and prevent burnout, which is key to the success of any personal project.

The right niche for you is the kind of setting that harmonizes with your essential, original personality. A restorative niche for a pseudo-extravert, for example, would provide quiet and reduced stimulation. In contrast, a natural extravert, called upon to act out of character as an introvert, would require a restorative niche that was stimulating and engaging—preferably with lots of other extraverts who would be extraverting themselves with great vigor. Karaoke, anyone?

One of our doctoral students at the University of Cambridge, Sanna Balsari-Palsule, has been investigating the nature and function of restorative niches at two different companies.[31] Participants completed a measure of Big Five traits that assessed both their "natural" traits and those they enacted at work. This allowed us to assess the extent to which they were engaging in free traits. They were also given a general description of restorative niches and asked to describe what kinds of niches they used in their workplaces. Her results are intriguing. She found that the restorative niches fell into five categories:

FORMS OF RESTORATIVE NICHE	EXAMPLES	FREQUENCY
People	"lunch with colleagues," "chatting in the kitchen," "go for lunch with interesting people," "time with friends"	59
Places	"sit in the sun," "breakroom," "shutting myself in a meeting room," "quiet rooms"	19
Activities	"Ping-Pong," "short five-minute breaks," "read a book during my lunch break," "go for a walk in the park," "drawing," "go for coffee"	41
Health/ Body	"gym," "running in Regent's Park," "meditation," "yoga"	24
Technology	"listening to music," "YouTube," "surfing the Internet," "my blog"	39

Interacting with other people was the most dominant restorative niche reported, especially getting together with others at lunch, which was mentioned equally by introverts and extraverts. However, introverts preferred to go to lunch alone or with a maximum of one or two colleagues, while extraverts on average reported eating with four others. One extreme participant listed having eighty lunch partners!

Activities were also frequently mentioned as restorative niches and involved a mixture of indoor activities like foosball and pool (available on the premises) and running. But even though many people engaged in the same activity, there were subtle differences reflecting personality. Extraverts were more likely to report "running club" and introverts just "running."

The notion of free traits has been studied primarily with the Big Five dimension of extraversion, but I believe it applies to other traits as well. Recall Victoria? She is naturally agreeable and kind but needs to be strategically pushy, assertive, and disruptive in order to find a safe place for her ailing mother. After all that head-butting, Victoria may need a restorative niche where she can regain her natural affability. It may be simply chilling with gentle people who would never think of themselves as comprising a restorative niche. But I suspect they would find the prospect a most agreeable one.

It's important to understand how restorative niches work because, when we act out of character, our environments might afford us the opportunity to return to our "natural" state. Or—and here is where you are empowered to support yourself—we may *create* new restorative niches on our own. This trick is especially important, considering the kind of power our environments can have over our endeavors.

What kinds of niches would be most restorative for you? Is it a hip-hop dance class or a long swim in a cold ocean? Is it dinner with ten friends or a solo hike in the forest?

As a biogenic introvert I have had my own challenges in finding restorative niches, particularly after having acted out of character as a pseudo-extraverted professor. One of the most rewarding things in my life is to engage with students. Particularly with students who are highly combustible, I work hard in my lectures to throw out sparks. I act out of character. This can be exhausting. So during breaks, I will retreat to my office, or the men's room, or occasionally a broom closet, in order to give a lucid second half to my lecture. Once, I inadvertently locked myself in the closet. That restorative niche didn't restore me for long.

As for your own restorative resources, they become most apparent when everyday constraints are lifted and you can act spontaneously. Perhaps catching some time to read a short book that helps you better understand your personality fits the bill just fine. If so, I'm happy you picked this particular niche.

3 Personal Contexts: The Social Ecology of Project Pursuit

Let's say that by now you've got a manageable, meaningful set of personal projects that are neatly aligned with your inborn traits. Can you look forward with confidence, sure of smooth sailing ahead? Not so fast; biogenic traits aren't the only forces that can help or hinder you. The world around you also plays a vital role in your pursuit of personal projects. But here again, you have power. You needn't sit passively by as external circumstances buffet your projects about. Just as you can pick up a free trait to overcome your biological first nature, you can actively alter your environment to clear a path for your personal projects.

Take a closer look at your social environment, and you'll see that some parts of it are relatively fixed and some parts are flexible. The fixed features might be things like the demographics of your city or the topography of your neighborhood. The more dynamic personal features might be which neighbors you choose to befriend and the transportation you use to get around town. The distinction between the stable and dynamic features is that the former are objective realities: the fact that you live in a high-density city. The latter are how you personally view and interact with that context: you find the crush of people lively and exciting or smothering and claustro-phobic; you develop a particular daily routine; you find your niche within the urban jungle.[32]

These dynamic features are what I call the *personal contexts* of your life. They are external environments—physical, geo-graphical, cultural, social—that you can influence through your own actions and attitudes. The stable features of your social ecology are difficult for you to change, but personal contexts are malleable. Bend them to better support your personal projects, and you take greater command of your flourishing or floundering.

Let's start with how your personal projects work within your environment—what are the various influences and where do the flexible, personal contexts lie? These might range from the micro-level influence of people and places in your immediate environment to the middle-level influence of the organizations where you work and play, to the more distant influences, such as your political, historical, and economic contexts. So, let's see how we can configure our environment to most effectively pursue our personal projects.

Close-Up: Projects with Others

Consider your own personal projects right now. Are they mainly solitary pursuits? Are they primarily pursued with an intimate partner? Are they shared with scores of loving friends whom you can't see enough of? Clearly your stable personality traits will determine which of these ways of doing your projects is most congenial. But for those of us who are not recluses or hermits or monks of a certain order, other people figure importantly in our daily pursuits. How does this play out?

Those whose personal projects are carried out exclusively with one other person are potentially vulnerable. We have studied these close-up aspects of project pursuit by looking at how many other people are involved in a person's projects. One of the important issues here is whether you have a diversity of individuals with whom you share your projects, or whether they are instead all focused on only one person. You can look at your own projects in this way. For each of your projects list the names of others who are involved in it.[33]

My research team and I have found considerable variation in how people respond to this question. There are some who are, or think they are, sole proprietors of their personal projects. They list no other people as being involved. Others list a diversity of individuals typically spread across different categories of projects, such as professional, recreational, or domestic pursuits. But there are some for whom all projects are carried out with the same person. That's risky. If everything you do is with Chris, then what would happen to your project system if Chris, for whatever reason, were to disappear? Just as removal of a core project can be massively disruptive to the structure of a person's life, so would the absence of the one person who has been with you throughout all your pursuits. The death of a loved one, the breakup of a marriage, or the treachery of a business partner is painful enough; the collapse of shared projects can amplify that pain.

We have also looked at how other people influence the success of our core personal projects. In one study, we looked at pregnancy as a personal project and how it unfolded throughout the months preceding and including delivery. We examined how successful the birthing experience was, not just in terms of the mother's personal experience but also in terms of medical appraisal of the child's physical wellness (Apgar scores). The best single predictor of both measures was the emotional support of the mother's partner. A second study examined the factors leading to success among entrepreneurs in the start-up year of their projects. Once again we measured both subjective feelings of success and more objective indicators like financial success. We found that the best predictor of both kinds of success was the emotional support of the entrepreneur's partner. We often hear entrepreneurs talk about one of their precious upstarts as "their baby." It is a metaphor, of course, but we can acknowledge the emotional equivalence readily. The support of the partner can make delivery of something splendid even better.[34]

In relationships, project pursuit can be a delicate dance. One key finding from early research with personal projects was that intimate partners were not only the major facilitators of our projects, but also the major source of frustration.[35] Sometimes it's just a matter of timing. Let's say you like to jog as soon as you get home from work. It is one of the most rewarding recurring projects in your life. It relaxes and restores you. But it is precisely when you get home from work that your partner most wants to just decompress with you and talk about how the day has gone, how your toddler had a standoff with the stupid cat, and how you are missed during the day. But you didn't realize he felt that way until he happened to drop it into a conversation almost inadvertently. Those are small things worth being sensitive about. It might be no big deal for you to delay the jog by half an hour, and this slight change in time may benefit you both.

There is another way you could deal with this: get your partner to join you in jogging! He might enjoy it, and you can catch up on life during the jog. As a bonus, it might fortify your relationship. Of course, jogging is just one example. Perhaps you love rock collecting, camping, or doing the tango. Whatever the passion, a study of the personal projects of individuals in long-term romantic relationships found that the larger the number of shared projects between partners the stronger and longer lasting those relationships were.[36]

So, in sum, there are various ways you can shape your closest social environment to support your projects. Choose a diverse set of people to share your projects with, communicate clearly about what matters to you, share projects wholeheartedly with the most important people—and you grant yourself a greater chance of success. Of course our social environment is rather more complex than this in real life. If you both go jogging, who is looking after your toddler? Your neurotic cat?

Do you have support from outside the house? Are you in the

kind of community where neighbors readily volunteer to look after things? Does your workplace provide the kind of flextime that would make all these daily project challenges more manageable? We are about to move up a level in our scanning of your social ecology. We might choose to examine the context of your office, your school, your extended family, your neighborhood, or your circle of friends—all of these fit into the middle-distance realm of your environment. To take just one example, let's look at your workplace.

Middle-Distance: Projects at Work

Several years ago, Susan Phillips and I examined the impact of the features of the daily work environment (work climate) on the personal projects of senior managers in private- and public-sector organizations.[37] We wanted to know if certain work environments were more supportive of personal projects than others. At first there appeared to be gender differences. For women, there was a substantial link between how they thought their personal projects were going and various aspects of their work climate, such as the absence of conflict, how supportive it was, and how much autonomy it granted its workers. For men, the link was virtually absent. The success men had in their personal projects had little to do with the conditions they had encountered at work. Why? As we began exploring why these gender differences occurred, we discovered that another factor seemed to be at play.

In governmental organizations, the women were in the

minority (only about 13 percent of senior managers at the time), and most had not been in their positions as long as their male counterparts. Perhaps it was a "minority" or "newcomer" phenomenon—people who felt they were particularly visible because they stood out as different, or who were relatively new to the organization, needed to curtail their personal projects to fit with the organizational climate in a way that more seasoned individuals did not. Those who were learning the ropes were highly sensitive to the subtleties of organizational life and adjusted their projects so as to hew more closely to their office norms—a compromise that often didn't bode well for personal projects. This explanation gained plausibility when we looked at one of the government organizations in which the senior positions were more equally balanced by gender. There, the differences between men and women disappeared.

That is not to say, however, that men and women thrive equally in all kinds of environments. There was one gender effect, however, that did seem to hold across the public and private sectors. In describing their preferred organizational climate for pursuing their projects, women placed "allows me to connect with others" as a high priority. Men did not. For men, the most desirable work climate was one in which they could pursue their projects without any impedance. A "clear the deck, I'm coming through" atmosphere was perfect for them. Of course, if they are all coming through in simultaneous pursuit of their singular projects, the deck is going to get pretty chaotic. Discretion among deckhands is required.

Knowing the potent influence of a workplace on your projects (even projects that take place outside the office), you can act to control what aspects of it you can. Consider company culture when choosing jobs, or propose office policies that support workers in pursuing full lives. Test the winds, change course, change your attitude toward your crewmates, or, if all else fails, jump ship.

Zooming High: Intimate Projects and Political Culture

Zoom out further, and you see how even the broadest contexts, those embedded in our culture, can affect our most intimate endeavors. At this level it becomes clear that we are influenced, sometimes quite dramatically, by the political, economic, and historical contexts of our lives. Our deepest aspirations for ourselves and those we love may be encouraged and supported by these contexts—or systematically undermined.

The best example of these influences is the research of David Frost at the University of Surrey. Frost adopted the social ecological framework to examine the intimate projects of heterosexual and LGBT individuals. His results were very thought-provoking.[38] He began by soliciting a listing of the intimate personal projects that they were pursuing. Here is a sampling of the personal projects that were elicited:

Meet some new people and go on dates with them
Meet a guy with a career
Making Matt feel more special

Packing/moving to our new apartment
Get reunited geographically with my boyfriend within a year
Improving communication with my girlfriend
Being in love with Tom
Planning to get married
Improve the quality of sex in my relationship
Spending quality time with my husband
Not picking fights with Jeanette
Helping my girlfriend get through chemo
Trying to prevent my impending divorce by going through a
    temporary separation
Get over my ex-lover's betrayal

Frost was able to demonstrate that, contrary to some stereotypes about the intimate pursuits of sexual-minority people, their intimacy projects were just as meaningful as for the heterosexual majority. They were as self-expressive, congruent with their values, and important in their lives. Where there were significant differences, however, was in the manageability of intimate projects—people from minority groups appraised their intimate projects as less likely to progress satisfactorily and come to fruition.

Barriers to the pursuit of intimate projects appeared at the everyday level of social interaction, where the subtle and not-so-subtle signs of discrimination against LGBT individuals were all too apparent. But the most intriguing finding of Frost's research is how it reveals the impact of the political systems in which these projects are pursued. By examining the postal codes for where the study participants lived, he discovered that in some jurisdictions sexual-minority groups reported significantly more barriers to pursuing their most intimate projects. In those jurisdictions where there was greater recognition of LGBT rights, including civil union and especially marriage, the intimacy projects of LGBT individuals were perceived as both meaningful and achievable. They flourished. In contrast, in other jurisdictions, the intimate concerns of sexual minorities floundered. Consider the force of the impact there despite the distance between cause and effect; large, macro-level political forces can forestall the expression and frustrate the sustainable pursuit of even the most intimate aspirations.

The study of personal projects does, however, provide some encouraging signs that determined action can provoke change. In Frost's study, the barriers created by interpersonal and political forces applied distinctively to intimacy projects. In more public realms, such as work or recreational projects, there was no evidence that the LGBT people Frost studied faced special barriers. This is unlikely to have been the case even a decade ago in most Western industrialized countries.

So here is cause for hope. Although politics are fairly stable influences on project pursuit, such forces should not be seen as immutable. We can change those forces by the concerted acts of those who care—such as the push by activists for several decades to win legal protection and social acceptance for sexual minorities. The political and the personal are intimately related, and transformational change can be brought about for both.

When I read Frost's findings and then joined him in writing

about this research, I had an uncanny feeling of déjà vu. It reminded me of a skinny Canadian standing outside the administration building at UC Berkeley learning that change was possible. It still is.

4 The Myth of Authenticity: The Challenge of Being Oneself

A half century ago, when Ted Sarbin asked me "Who are you?" I had a mock-serious answer, meant more to engage discussion than to comment on my identity. But let's add "really" to the end of the question, and ask it of you:

"Who are you, *really*?"

Do you want to dodge the question, as I did with Sarbin? I hope not, because this amended query ups the ante and calls for serious self-reflection. It means you are being asked to search through all your different identities and declare one that is closest to the truth, or to come up with an answer that is nearest to your core self. And crucially, it implies that there is a *real* you—an authentic you—and that you should seek it.

There is perhaps no more frequently offered advice that we give to others who are making a hard decision than "Just be yourself." But in many ways this is not a particularly helpful piece of advice, in part because it is vague but also because, as controversial as this may sound, it may not actually be in the person's best interests.[39]

Before we go ahead and dismantle traditional views of authenticity, let's briefly examine how traditional views of authenticity are dominating discussions in contemporary society. The buzz about authenticity recently hit boardrooms and management schools around the globe, with "authentic leadership" becoming a hot topic for seminars and company workshops. The reason for its popularity is perfectly clear: The financial crisis and ethics scandals that created such havoc in the past decade prompted a major reassessment of what it takes to be a good leader—honesty and transparency. Leaders need to speak clearly and without artifice. They can't play games, and they must be genuine. They need to be authentic.[40]

If being authentic is to be real and honest and full of integrity, surely this is something you, too, should aspire to, right? It's not quite that simple.

I believe that the search for authenticity is somewhat misguided—that there is, in fact, no one true you. In fact, you can have *multiple authenticities.* In an era that puts so much weight on the idea of one true self, this is a complex and controversial notion, but having multiple authenticities doesn't imply that we lack a moral compass or that we are disingenuous or even particularly conflicted. It simply means that being a sincere person can mean different things at different times, and that who you are *really* might differ depending on the circumstance.

When Authenticity Fails

While openness and transparency can be a powerful means of connecting us with others, authenticity is not always a panacea. Herminia Ibarra, a business professor in France, has written a provocative and insightful analysis of how authenticity in leadership may not be the unmitigated good that many organizations believe it is. She argues that totally revealing oneself, warts and all, may detract from, not enhance, one's capacity to lead.[41]

She gives the example of Cynthia, a general manager in the healthcare field who had been given a major promotion. The new position greatly increased the scope and complexity of her responsibilities. This was a daunting challenge, and she could have simply steeled herself to it and faked confidence. Instead, she opted to be completely authentic. She believed in the benefits of transparency and collaborative leadership. So, as Ibarra puts it, "she bared her soul to her new employees: 'I want to do this job,' she said, 'but it's scary, and I need your help.' Her candor backfired; she lost credibility with people who wanted and needed a confident leader to take charge."

Cynthia's case is an intriguing example in light of our earlier discussion about free traits. She displayed aspects of her natural disposition toward anxiety, thinking this would be well received as honest. Unfortunately, she was perceived as weak instead. What if Cynthia had considered creating the appearance of stability? By enacting a free trait of pseudo-stability, she could have gained the confidence and commitment of those who worked for her. She could have advanced her core project for the company. And by practicing the habits and behaviors of stability, she might have *truly become* more stable once she felt bolstered by her coworkers' faith in her leadership.

I imagine this "fake it till you make it" strategy can, at first blush, feel disingenuous to some. But I believe that changing your personality to match different situations isn't inauthentic at all. Here's why: Calls for total authenticity rest on the assumption that any outward behavior that's out of sync with our inward feelings is dishonest. Free traits, from this perspective, are lies. But I urge you to question that very assumption. Restricting ourselves to being only oneself can forestall the possibility of being something more.

I suspect that some of you might generally agree with the notion that always being "you" is constraining and limits our capacity for growth. Others, however, will be very uncomfortable with this idea. So it is helpful here to consider another trait of personality that clarifies whether you are sympathetic to the notion of multiple authenticities. The concept is called self-monitoring, and it looks at precisely this tendency to favor showing fidelity to oneself or flexibility to the demands of the situations we confront.[42]

Self-Monitoring and Authenticity

To gauge where you fall on the self-monitoring scale, consider these statements:

1. I find it easy to imitate the behavior of other people.
2. In different situations and with different people, I often act like very different persons.
3. I'm not always the person I appear to be.

If you strongly agreed with each of these statements, you are likely to be a high self-monitor. That means you pay close attention to how you behave in different situations, varying your behavior in response to the environment around you. If you said no to each of these questions, you are probably a low self-monitor. One of your most characteristic features is that you are yourself in all situations. You don't create a new self to adapt to the particular situation you find yourself in.

To understand how these tendencies play out day to day, imagine you're a low self-monitor in a relationship with a high self-monitor. Your partner, from your perspective, is a bit of a stand-up chameleon. She appears to be different people in different situations—a corporate self, a party self, a playing-with-the-kids self, and you end up being confused. Who is this person to whom I'm so committed? Which of the many hers am I really in love with? And when your partner looks at you, there is also confusion but a very different kind. You are seen as constant and predictable, which certainly has its comforts. But that constancy can be seen as rather boring and, worse, unduly rigid. Why can't you be flexible and accommodate to the situation? It's a dinner party! Couldn't you just submit to the fun of the situation and be a tiny bit playful for one evening instead of expatiating, repeatedly, on the fiscal benefits of a flat tax?

Substantial research indicates that high self-monitors tend to do well in several areas of life, but not so well in others. One area of strength for high self-monitors is work. If you are an adaptable sort, a high self-monitor, you are more likely than the low self-monitors you know to get promoted and assume leadership positions. You do well, in part, because you can play diverse roles that bridge different groups and alliances. But there's a downside for your organization: Unlike low self-monitors who are more strongly committed to their workplaces, you are more likely to bolt if a more congenial offer presents itself.[43] As you might imagine, this relative lack of commitment has consequences for the other major domain of life pursuit—your relationships. High self-monitors, relative to low, have less stable relationships.[44]

But—and here I am going to turn a number of old "be yourself" maxims on their heads—neither high nor low self-monitors are any more or less authentic than the other.

Mark Snyder, the originator of self-monitoring theory, has suggested that low self-monitors are principled, while high self-monitors are pragmatic. I think this is partially right. Are you a low self-monitor? Then you seek clarity about who you are and what you value. This clearly is a principled approach to your life. But it is also pragmatic; it prevents you from having to constantly decide who you ought to be in this situation or that role, freeing you to get on with the projects and aspirations you value. Are you a high self-monitor? Then your focus is on the practical demands of living in a complex world. This includes having to get along with different people with different expectations and rising to diverse occasions as needed. That, clearly, is pragmatic. But I think there is also a principled side to being a high self-monitor. You may value friendship or harmony, or being attentive to the needs of others. And if your clear presentation of a unified self gets lost in the process, that is fine with you—in fact, all the better.

Of course, the most likely answer is that you don't come down clearly on one side or the other. You are attuned to your

self-presentation in some contexts and oblivious to it in others. In fact, our research finds that self-monitoring is not fixed, like a biogenic trait, but dynamic, like a free trait. You use it when it's helpful in pursuing your personal projects.[45]

Viewing the vagaries of behavior this way is important. Not only does it help us better understand our fellow (confusing) humans, but it encourages us to look differently at authenticity itself. If consistency is not always the only moral path, and if inconsistent behavior can be both principled and pragmatic, then authenticity is not a singular thing. In fact, there are alternative ways of being authentic, and these are not fixed traits of people but flexible strategies for engaging with ourselves and the world.

Three Ways of Doing Authenticity

There are three fundamental ways in which we can answer the authenticity question, the "Who are you, *really*?" probe, corresponding to the different sources of personality—biogenic, sociogenic, and idiogenic—with which we are already familiar.

Biogenic Authenticity: Doing What Comes Naturally

One way in which you can be authentic is to show fidelity to your biogenic self—the self that is determined by your physical makeup. Imagine, for example, right now that your phone rings with an invitation to a neighborhood party next weekend. What is your immediate, unscripted gut-feel? Is it delight because you love parties, or apprehension because you find them invariably draining? If you act on the basis of your first-nature preferences, you are showing biogenic authenticity—fidelity to your natural self. If asked, you justify your decision to go or to stay home by saying that you do what comes *naturally*. You're genuine; you don't fake it. You love parties, or you hate parties, but the "you" who is doing the loving or hating is the authentic you. This is classic low self-monitoring.

Biogenic first-nature preferences are intimately related to our relatively stable traits. The open and extraverted individual is likely to have a spontaneous "Let's go!" response to the invitation. The neurotic, introverted person will almost reflexively say, "Ah, sorry, no—I'm busy that night" (perhaps adding, sotto voce, "and for the next seven years").

Sociogenic Authenticity: Doing One's Duty

But when it comes to going to the party, you might also show fidelity to the sociogenic demands that arise from the cultural norms and situations that shape your daily behavior. Irrespective of your personality traits, your decision to decline or accept the invitation may depend on whether you are, say, a member of an ultraconservative religious group that looks at parties as frivolous. Or you may be on the executive committee of the neighborhood association, and it is, after all, a neighborhood event. Without thinking, you decide on the basis of what you *ought* to do according to social convention, not necessarily what you *want* to do. It is entirely possible that what you desire and what you believe to be required may be in harmony, in which case your action is doubly determined.

Beyond the scale of the neighborhood, our identities can be scripted by cultural conventions expressed in the media or in literature. This notion is called the Quixotic Principle, introduced to the field of psychology in 1994 by none other than Ted Sarbin. It holds that scripts or templates in our culture tell us how to behave and how to comport ourselves in our daily lives. These rules of conduct are powerful and pervasive. The most poignant example of this influence was Don Quixote, Miguel de Cervantes's compelling character, a simple man from La Mancha who, entranced by tales of the knights-errant of an earlier time, set out in search of great deeds and knightly virtue. He took his social scripts and templates from an earlier era. That his pursuits were sheer folly to those with whom he came in contact was of no consequence to him. In his mind, he was doing his duty.

Idiogenic Authenticity: The Deeper You

Let's return to the party: You walk in the door and spot one of your neighbors, Diego, who is there with his wife, Emily. For the past month you have run into Diego, always with Emily, at several social events. Given his conviviality and engagement at these functions, you assume he must be a rather extraverted person. When it comes to parties, you assume, Diego is a natural.

But it may well be that Diego is not a natural in the biogenic sense; in fact, he is extremely introverted and prefers to keep to himself and avoid the challenge of social situations. And there may not be any particular sociogenic norm that impels him to go to every major social event that month. In fact, both Diego and Emily are overworked associates at a firm that demands sixty-hour workweeks and total, unswerving devotion. There is no cultural expectation that coerces them to such extensive social engagement—quite the opposite. So for Diego, it is neither in his first nor second nature to party so heartily.

But his actions that month may well be an aspect of his *third* nature—the core personal projects of Diego's life. Emily is terminally ill, but she and Diego have decided not to let anyone but their closest family members know this. Her symptoms will progress rapidly, but at this point, she is still able to carry out routine activities and even some of the things she adores—like meeting with neighbors and catching up on things that matter to them. She loves parties—indeed, she lives for them.

For Diego, the most important project on the planet is "be there for Emily" and nothing will stop his commitment to this project. If it means that he needs to go against his first nature, fine. If it interferes with his work schedule and he lets down his firm, fine. Sometimes one pursuit claims our whole concentration and allegiance. The impending death of a loved one can certainly concentrate the mind.

So is Diego being inauthentic? I don't think so. He is pushing against his biogenic traits, ignoring the sociogenic pressures of his life, and showing utter fidelity to his core project.

When we see the complete social-ecological picture of who we are, it becomes clear that we can have multiple authenticities.

And it's natural for some of those authenticities to conflict. This does not mean we are adrift in a world of moral relativism but simply that there is more than one way of being a good person—and, crucially, of becoming a better person. It is by acknowledging all of our *selves* and adaptively weighing and rebalancing them that we can be truly authentic. Then we can best understand who we are and how best to engage our complex lives with integrity.

5 Well-Doing: The Sustainable Pursuit of Core Projects

In the end, we return to two pivotal questions: Who are you? and How are you doing? The first concerns your identity and personality; the second, whether your life is going well. And we've concluded that each of these is intimately related to the personal projects you are pursuing.

In this final chapter, I want to focus on how we can do something about our current lives and our future prospects. Our well-being may arise out of forces over which we have little control, such as our biogenic traits and our social environments. But here I want to focus on how we can improve the quality of our lives. I call this *well-doing*. Well-doing is the process by which we can create flourishing in our lives by sustainably pursuing our core personal projects.

Core Projects: The Source of What Matters to Us

All personal projects matter, but not all personal projects matter equally. Take another look at your list of personal projects. Maybe it includes "empty the dishwasher" alongside "complete the marathon," or "don't dominate the office karaoke party" right next to "look for a better job." Some of these projects are more transitory and peripheral to your sense of who you are. Others are core and self-defining.

Core projects are those that affect all your other projects. To determine whether each of your projects is core or peripheral, ask yourself this question: What impact would it have on your other projects if this project were to succeed or fail? If a core project succeeds everything else goes well for you; if it doesn't, your whole system can collapse.

Another important question to ask in determining which projects are core is whether you are open to changing them, or even giving them up. When your core projects are challenged, you will resist changing them, often with astonishing resolve. Take, for example, "train for my next marathon." If this project disappears, it may or may not implicate change in a runner's other projects. They may be essentially independent of running. But what if running the marathon is intimately and extensively linked with the rest of the runner's projects—keeping healthy, feeling a sense of accomplishment, looking good, having control over one's life. Each of those articulated or tacit projects may, on probing, be linked to running. The runner's whole sense of self may be wrapped around the identity of being a marathoner. It plays a vital role in the sense of who she is and how her life is progressing. But this kind of core project pursuit creates some vulnerability. What if there is an accident? She's running along smoothly and elegantly one morning when suddenly a pothole appears, a twist, a fall, and in an instant her ankle is broken right along with her heart.

Having core projects is why you get up in the morning. They bring meaning and significance and direction to our lives and, ultimately, define who we are. Indeed, Bernard Williams, a philosopher who has thought deeply about this subject, has speculated that without such projects in our lives we may be inclined to wonder if it is worth carrying on at all. Fortunately, even when our most cherished projects are derailed or demolished, we have the capacity to rebuild our lives with new projects and commitments, and facing the day becomes inviting again.[46]

Internal Sustainability of Project Pursuit

What are your core projects? Examine the list you created and identify those that are most central to your personal project system—those that are interlinked with your other projects. You may not have been consciously aware of their centrality until you began to question what would happen if they disappeared from your life. In many respects, a core project is the most self-defining of your projects, the one that is your trademark, your most singular pursuit—the one that defines who you are *for you*. What internal factors might help you keep that project alive, or the absence of which might lead to it being abandoned or grow stale? The following are a few important ones to keep in mind.

Biogenic alignment: Aligning your core projects with your biogenic traits increases their sustainability. A quiet, introverted person pursuing a core project of "continue writing my poetry"

is more likely to sustain that project than if he is aspiring to "run for political office." A person low in conscientiousness is not as likely to sustain a project of "complete my PhD" as one who is conscientious. Despite a burning resolve to liberate his people, a highly neurotic individual may find the struggle so oppressively arduous that he simply can't sustain it for a protracted period. Which isn't to say that you should only engage in those projects that are consistent with your biogenic traits—indeed, our discussion of free traits expressly encourages you to step out of your comfort zone to advance concerns that matter to you. But in terms of long-term pursuit, it means that the path will be smoother and the costs less onerous if there is broad agreement between your traits and the projects you are undertaking.

Make them public: A powerful way of enhancing the likelihood of our projects progressing well is the commitment that we make to them. Project commitment has two faces. Inwardly, we can devote ourselves to a course of action, which leads us to give it priority and invest it with a deeper sense of meaning. But commitment also has an outer face: When we pledge to a project and other people are aware of this, it is far more likely to succeed. By making your core projects known to others, especially your partners and loved ones, you help bring into play their support and encouragement.

Interestingly, men and women differ over which projects they find easy to make visible to others. Men, for example, find that when they make stressful projects visible, their projects become vulnerable, whereas women show the reverse pattern—publicizing stressful projects makes them less vulnerable. It could be that, for men, revealing stressful projects conveys weakness, at least in their eyes; for women, it serves to stimulate support from others.

Reframe your goals: Remember George Kelly and the psychology of personal constructs? Kelly believed that our personal constructs—the conceptual goggles through which we view the world—provide a way of ordering our lives. But while personal constructs are our frames for structuring our days, they can also be the cages we lock ourselves in by perseverating in the way we look at the world. In short, the way you construe your personal projects may have a significant impact on whether their pursuit is sustainable. For example, if you listed some version of the personal project "lose weight," you are not alone. It is the most frequently listed project we see in our research. However, construing the project in those terms is associated with less long-term success than if it were phrased "enjoy myself at the gym."[47] Reframing your personal projects by slightly changing the way you phrase them boosts their sustainability, helping you reach your goal.

Strategic Imbalance: Prioritizing What We Do When
There is much written about the need for work-life balance as a way of minimizing the stress of multiple demands. But sometimes balance is not possible—the demands of your professional life call for a sustained period of action. Or a child's sickness simply can't be ignored. In both cases you give priority to a project that comes with a sense of urgency and importance that requires you to be strategically unbalanced.

Your other projects, neglected for the moment, can return to the forefront at a later time.

External Sustainability of Project Pursuit

Whereas internal sustainability refers to our ability to control our motivation and commitment to our core projects, we also require external sustainability of those pursuits. This involves managing our everyday contexts or social ecologies, which include not only the physical environments around us but also other individuals and institutions. Consider the following sampling of the ways in which we can cultivate our surroundings, from our personal networks to our local communities and larger societies. Each of these can influence whether our core projects are sustainable. And each of these can be changed.

Micro-Level: Nurturing Our Nurturers

We have seen how the emotional support of others is critical to project success, so it is important that we establish the conditions that will sustain the support. Sometimes while pursuing our core projects we are so vigilantly aware of the barriers we need to overcome and the self-motivation we need to keep up the pursuit that we forget to acknowledge those who have been supporting us all along. And once more, the support from others may be something you don't recognize until it is withdrawn. Whether it is a formal gratitude letter or a more informal and subtle "Thanks, I couldn't do this without you," giving value to those who bolster our core pursuits is fundamental to our sustaining them.

Middle-Level: Shaping Our Personal Contexts

As we have seen, the daily contexts of our lives can facilitate or frustrate project pursuit and subvert the possibility of living a flourishing life. There is no more gripping example than the current refugee crisis and its horrifying impact on the lives of those displaced and desperate to live better lives. However, even in trying circumstances, middle-level contexts—the local communities we're a part of—can be creatively changed.

In a much earlier refugee crisis, that in Southeast Asia in the late 1970s, my student Pit-Fong Loh and I had the opportunity to study how the so-called boat people fared when they arrived in North America. We found that the best predictor of whether or not they flourished was the extent to which language was a barrier to the sustainability of their core projects. To help the refugees remove that barrier by learning English, we set up a local "personal project exchange" program in which people who spoke English would help those wanting help with English in exchange for such things as Vietnamese cooking classes or other services. Participants in the exchange reported that the experience was not only practically helpful to their core pursuits, but also led to new friendships.

There are myriad ways of optimizing your context, from forming a neighborhood association in which neighbors look out for each other to petitioning the city for a new bus route. By making your core projects more viable, as we helped refugees do through the project exchange, you can move from merely surviving toward flourishing.

Macro-Level: Large-Scale Change

Without a doubt, the highest level contexts—those big, overarching forces of politics and culture—influence the way we approach our personal projects. In some political systems, it is possible to engage in one's core projects with minimal interference. In others, some projects are simply proscribed as "don't even think about it." Whether it is the pursuit of education for girls or the ability of a gay couple to get married, some of the most compelling and intimate aspirations can be thwarted by a society's rules before they even begin. But political regimes can be changed, though it may be a protracted and bloody prospect. One of the most interesting aspects of David Frost's research on the intimacy projects of nonheterosexual couples was seeing how active they were in agitating for legislation that would provide support for marriage among sexual minorities. When intensely personal goals converge with political activism, the seemingly impenetrable obstacles to pursuing core projects can be dismantled.

Woven into all these strategies for successful project pursuit is an essential lesson. If you remember none of the specific tips I've discussed, retain this: By examining your core projects and how they can be sustained you will increase your power to change the trajectory of your life.

And yet what if you are a bit resistant to enact change? Perhaps you have a ready and easy answer to "Who are you?"

(same old me) and "How are you doing?" (not too badly). If this is so, I want to relate a comment George Kelly made about such an approach to life:

"A good deal is said these days about being oneself.... This strikes me as a very dull way of living; in fact, I would be inclined to argue that all of us would be better off if we set out to be something other than what we are. Well, I'm not so sure we would all be better off—perhaps it would be more accurate to say life would be a lot more interesting."[48]

The Bearable Lightness of Well-Doing

We've come a long way in understanding who you are. We've seen how forces arising out of your biogenic disposition, your first nature, shape your personality. We've seen how the sociogenic influences of culture and society, your second nature, also exert great influence. And we have concluded that your personal projects, the expression of your third nature, the prospective you, can help you transcend those two forces. We examined how the sustainable pursuit of core projects are central to human flourishing. Ultimately, we found that the most illuminating measure of our well-being is not well-being at all but well-doing—a concept rooted in the notion of agency, in the idea that we have influence over who we are and how successfully our life is going. In the end, that may have been the truth I told Ted Sarbin I was seeking all those years ago, however ironically I had expressed it at the time.

Now, you may think I'm suggesting that the key to human flourishing is concertedly structuring your life through meticulously chosen projects. In order to be happy, you must control and finesse and regiment your daily actions. You must always have a sense of direction, your eyes constantly on the prize. Such personal crafting is a considerable advance over a life spent in resigned discontentment about how the genetic lottery or your miserable living conditions have cheated you. But adhering to it with total regimentation could also be exhausting.

Instead, I'd like to leave you with one final piece of advice—one that may seem surprising: Embrace the unexpected.

Amid all this conscious shaping of our future prospects, there also needs to be room for serendipity in our lives. We must be alive to new encounters, open to being gobsmacked by something that brings unexpected delight. Such lightness, I believe, is essential to ensuring the sustainable pursuit of our deepest concerns—and to developing new ones. It is what allows our humanity to shine through.

It is entirely possible to pursue our projects conscientiously while being receptive to chance. So hone your skills as the athlete you always dreamed of becoming, but be ready to change course if you begin to demonstrate a strong passion for science. Keep writing your book of poetry, but seize the opportunity when an editor asks you to write an article on classical music. Plan your long-awaited trip to Vegas, but make the most of a night in Chicago when your flight is delayed. It is ultimately the marriage of these two approaches that makes life deeply fulfilling.

Go forth and pursue your projects. Make them meaningful and manageable, and connected to others. Let them harmonize with your essential nature wherever they can, and provide yourself a chance to recuperate when they demand that you act out of character for a while. Where society and culture support your efforts, embrace that boost; where they interfere, consider pressing society and culture to change. But while you're at it, now and again remember to release the sense of pursuit. Relax into the spontaneity of the moment, whatever it is. This lightness, this easing back, is essential if we are to carry on at all. Whimsy and humor can sustain us through the demanding pursuits of core projects, so encourage them. Loosen up. Maybe you could start by trying to lick your elbow. Or, even better, getting someone else to lick it.

The Big Five Inventory-2 Extra-Short Form*

Here are a number of characteristics that may or may not apply to you. For example, do you agree that you are someone who likes to spend time with others? Please write a number next to each statement to indicate the extent to which you agree or disagree with that statement.

---

1 DISAGREE STRONGLY

2 DISAGREE A LITTLE

3 NEUTRAL: NO OPINION

4 AGREE A LITTLE

5 AGREE STRONGLY

I am someone who . . .

_____ 1. tends to be quiet.

_____ 2. is compassionate, has a soft heart.

_____ 3. tends to be disorganized.

_____ 4. worries a lot.

_____ 5. is fascinated by art, music, or literature.

_____ 6. is dominant, acts as a leader.

_____ 7. is sometimes rude to others.

_____ 8. has difficulty getting started on tasks.

_____ 9. tends to feel depressed, blue.

_____ 10. has little interest in abstract ideas.

_____ 11. is full of energy.

_____ 12. assumes the best about people.

_____ 13. is reliable, can always be counted on.

_____ 14. is emotionally stable, not easily upset.

_____ 15. is original, comes up with new ideas.

Scoring Key:

Openness: Add up your scores for items 5 and 15 and subtract score for item 10.

Conscientiousness: Subtract your scores for items 3 and 8 from score for item 13.

Extraversion: Add up your scores for items 6 and 11 and subtract score for item 1.

Agreeableness: Add up your scores for items 2 and 12 and subtract score for item 7.

Neuroticism: Add up your scores for items 4 and 9 and subtract score for item 13.

Interpretation:

O: Average score is 5. Scores of 7+ are relatively high; 3 or less relatively low.

C: Average score is -1. Scores of 1+ are relatively high; -3 or less relatively low.

E: Average score is 4. Scores of 6+ are relatively high; 2 or less relatively low.

A: Average score is 6. Scores of 8+ are relatively high; 4 or less relatively low.

N: Average score is 3. Scores of 5+ are relatively high; 1 or less relatively low.

*The Big Five Inventory-2 Extra-Short Form (BFI-2-XS) items copyright 2015 by Oliver P. John and Christopher J. Soto. Reprinted with permission. For more information about the BFI-2, visit the Colby Personality Lab website at http://www.colby.edu/psych/personality-lab/.

ACKNOWLEDGMENTS

I am delighted to acknowledge the creative engagement of
the TED community with this book and with my linked TED
2016 talk. Special thanks to Susan Cain for her early advocacy
and to David Lavin, agent extraordinaire, for linking me with
TED Books. Michelle Quint and her team expertly guided
me through the process of writing and revision. By deft and
thoughtful editing they helped me avoid excessively academic
phrasing (Or, as I would prefer to say, "They helped me es-
chew obfuscation"). Chris Anderson, Kelly Stoetzel, Brian
Greene, and Helen Walters were generous in their support and
encouragement as I went through the surreal experience of
TEDification. To be part of their community is a giddy adventure. And my wife, Susan Phillips, as ever, provided the love,
advice, and support that sustained me through this core project.

Introduction

1   This was a collaborative project between Mark Rosenzweig and David Krech of the Department of Psychology and Marian Diamond of the Department of Anatomy at the University of California, Berkeley. See Rosenzweig, Krech, Bennett, & Diamond (1962).

2   The emerging field of social genomics has exciting implications for understanding health and flourishing. For example, Steve Cole and his colleagues at UCLA have demonstrated that how genes express themselves is linked to how much loneliness is experienced by participants in his studies. See Cole (2009).

Chapter 1

3   See Lone Frank (2011).

4   The term *pronoia* was first coined by the sociologist Fred Goldner and is meant to depict the characteristics that are the polar opposite to those of paranoia. See Goldner (1982).

5   There is now a substantial body of research on the Big Five traits. See especially the review by Ozer and Benet-Martínez (2006) that explores the practical consequences of traits for education, marriage, health, and work. Daniel Nettle (2007) has written an excellent introduction for the general reader. See also Little (2014), especially chapter 2.

6   An especially promising analysis of the neuropsychological basis of the Big Five traits appears in the work of Colin DeYoung and his colleagues. See DeYoung (2010).

7   See, for example, MacKinnon (1962) and Chapter 8 in Little (2014). For a detailed exposition of how the assessment process was carried out, see Serraino (2016).

8   See McCrae (2007).

9   See Hogan and Hogan (1993).

10   There is a vast research literature on extraversion and its effects on performance, motivation, and risk-taking. An authoritative and comprehensive review has been carried out by Wilt and Revelle (2008).

11   The study of frequency of intercourse was originally reported in Giese and

Schmidt (1968). I have been unable to find a more recent study, so I would caution the reader that these results were obtained from unmarried, heterosexual German university students who had reported being sexually active. And it was the sixties.

12   Little (1976) provides research on person-orientation, warmth, and expressiveness.

13   Elaine Aron has written perceptively about highly sensitive individuals who demonstrate some, but not all, of the characteristics of neurotics. Although more frequently associated with introversion, about 30 percent of highly sensitive individuals are extraverted. See Aron (1996).

14   The best source for reading about personal construct theory is still Kelly (1955).

15   I have given a more detailed treatment of the influence of personal construct theory on my own research elsewhere. See chapter 1 in Little, Salmela-Aro, and Phillips (2007).

Chapter 2

16   There is now an extensive research literature on Personal Projects Analysis. See Little (1983, 1998, 1999) and especially chapters 9 and 10 of Little (2014).

17   The prospective nature of human beings has been featured in a fascinating new book called *Homo Prospectus*. See Seligman, Railton, Baumeister, and Sripada (2016).

18   The question of what is a trivial pursuit is no trivial matter. "Walking the dog" is a more or less straightforward project for most of us, unless we don't have a dog. But if you are in a wheelchair, the dog is rambunctious, and the pavement is uneven, this is no trivial pursuit. A fair evaluation of another person's project needs to take both their aspirations and personal contexts into account. See Little (1989) for more details on this matter.

19   For details on the actual methods through which we do a detailed analysis of a personal project system, see Little and Gee (2007).

20   See Egan (2011).

21   See the work of Katariina Salmela-Aro, who initiated research on this topic (Salmela-Aro, 1992).

22   See Little (1989).

23   The foundational work on the effects of internally vs. externally regulated goal pursuit is contained in self-determination theory. See, for example, Deci and Ryan (2002).

24   Neil Chambers pioneered the linguistic analysis of the content of personal projects. See Chambers (2007).

25   For reviews of this, see Little (1989) and Little (1998).

26   This section draws heavily on Little, Lecci, and Watkinson (1992).

27   Preliminary evidence for the mediating role of project appraisals is found in Albuquerque, Lima, Matos, and Figueiredo (2012).

28   See the *Inside the Actors Studio* interview with Robin Williams at: https://www. youtube.com/watch?feature=player_embedded&v=AHOErukoKcI#at=12.

29   For more detailed accounts of free traits, see Little (2000) and Little and Joseph (2007).

30   The sociologist Arlie Hochschild conducted pioneering research on how professional roles require people to present themselves in ways that are emotionally managed rather than natural. See Hochschild (1983).

31   Sanna Balsari-Palsule's doctoral dissertation provides a rich source of information on free traits and the subtleties of restoration (Balsari-Palsule, 2016).

Chapter 3

32   The concepts of personal contexts and the social ecology of project pursuit are given detailed treatment in Little (1987, 1999, 2000, 2010).

33   See Paly and Little (1983).

34   I've discussed these studies, carried out by Nancy Keen and Craig Dowden, elsewhere (Little, 2014).

35   See Ruehlman and Wolchik (1988).

36   See Hwang (2004).

37   See Phillips, Little, and Goodine (1997).

38   See Frost (2011) and Little and Frost (2013).

Chapter 4

39   For a deeply insightful treatment by a philosopher on these questions, see *Against Authenticity: Why You Shouldn't Be Yourself* by Simon Feldman (2015).

40 See Thacker (2016).

41 See Ibarra (2015).

42 Mark Snyder developed the concept of self-monitoring. See Snyder (1987).

43 For details on self-monitoring in organizations, see Killduff and Day (1994).

44 See Snyder (1987).

45 See Little (2014), especially chapter 4.

Chapter 5

46 There is a provocative and growing research literature in philosophy on personal projects and their role in living a good life. Among the most important are Lomasky (1984), Betzler (2013), and Tiberius (2008). I have recently reviewed these perspectives on personal projects and well-doing (Little, 2016).

47 Michelle Segar, *No Sweat: How the Simple Science of Motivation Can Bring You a Lifetime of Fitness* (New York: AMACOM, 2015).

48 From Kelly (1964).

BIBLIOGRAPHY

Aron, Elaine N. *The Highly Sensitive Person.* New York: Broadway Books, 1996.

Balsari-Palsule, Sanna L. "The Artist Within the Actor: An Exploration of the Personal and Professional Consequences of Within-Individual Variation in Extraversion." PhD diss., University of Cambridge, 2016.

Betzler, Monika. "The Normative Significance of Personal Projects." In *Autonomy and the Self*, edited by Michael Kühler and Nadja Jelinek, 101–126. New York and Berlin: Springer, 2013.

Chambers, Neil C. "Just Doing It: Affective Implications of Project Phrasing." In *Personal Project Pursuit: Goals, Action, and Human Flourishing*, edited by Brian R. Little, Katariina Salmela-Aro, and Susan D. Phillips, 145–169. Mahwah, NJ: Lawrence Erlbaum Associates, 2007.

Cole, Steve. "Social Regulation of Human Gene Expression." *Current Directions in Psychological Science* 18 (2009): 132–137.

Deci, Edward L., and Richard M. Ryan. "Self-Determination Research: Reflections and Future Directions." In *Handbook of Self-Determination Research*, edited by Deci and Ryan, 431–441. Rochester, NY: University of Rochester Press, 2002.

DeYoung, Colin G. "Personality Neuroscience and the Biology of Traits." *Social and Personality Psychology Compass* 4 (2010): 1165–1180. doi:10.1111/j.1751-9004.2010.00327.

Egan, Jennifer. "To Do." *The Guardian.* July 22, 2011.

Feldman, Simon. *Against Authenticity: Why You Shouldn't Be Yourself.* London: Lexington Books, 2015.

Friedman, Howard S., Joan S. Tucker, Carol Tomlinson-Keasey, Joseph E. Schwartz, Deborah L. Wingard, and Michael H. Criqui. "Does Childhood Personality Predict Longevity?" *Journal of Personality and Social Psychology* 65, no. 1 (1993): 176–185.

Frost, David M. "Similarities and Differences in the Pursuit of Intimacy among Sexual Minority and Heterosexual Individuals: A Personal Projects Analysis." *Journal of Social Issues* 67, no. 2 (2011): 282–301.

Goldner, Fred. "Pronoia." *Social Problems* 30 (1982): 82–91.

Helliwell, John, Richard Layard, and Jeffrey Sachs, eds. *World Happiness Report: 2017.* New York: Earth Institute.

Hochschild, Arlie R. *The Managed Heart: Commercialization of Human Feeling.* Berkeley: University of California Press, 1983.

Hogan, Janice, and Robert Hogan. "The Ambiguity of Conscientiousness." Paper presented at the Eighth Annual Conference of the Society for Industrial and Organizational Psychology, San Francisco, CA, 1993.

Hudson, Nathan W., and Brent W. Roberts. "Goals to Change Personality Traits: Concurrent Links Between Personality Traits, Daily Behavior, and Goals to Change Oneself." *Journal of Research in Personality* 53 (2014): 68-83.

Hudson, Nathan W., and R. Chris Fraley. "Volitional Personality Trait Change: Can People Choose to Change Their Personality Traits?" *Journal of Personality and Social Psychology* 109 (2015): 490-507.

Hwang, Anne A. "Yours, Mine, Ours: The Role of Joint Personal Projects in Close Relationships." PhD diss., Harvard University, 2004.

Ibarra, Herminia. "The Authenticity Paradox." *Harvard Business Review.* January-February issue (2015).

Kelly, George A. *A Theory of Personality: The Psychology of Personal Constructs.* New York: W. W. Norton, 1955.

———. "The Language of Hypothesis: Man's Psychological Instrument." *Journal of Individual Psychology* 20 (1964): 137-152.

Kilduff, Martin, and David V. Day. "Do Chameleons Get Ahead? The Effects of Self-Monitoring on Managerial Careers." *Academy of Management Journal* 37, no. 4 (1994): 1047-1060.

Little, Brian R. "Specialization and the Varieties of Environmental Experience: Empirical Studies Within the Personality Paradigm." In *Experiencing the Environment*, edited by Seymour Wapner, Saul B. Cohen, and Bernard Kaplan, 81-116. New York: Plenum Press, 1976.

———. "Personality and the Environment." In *Handbook of Environmental Psychology*, edited by Daniel Stokols and Irwin Altman, 205-244. New York: Wiley, 1987.

———. "Personal Projects Analysis: Trivial Pursuits, Magnificent Obsessions, and the Search for Coherence." In *Personality Psychology: Recent Trends and Emerging Directions*, edited by David Buss and Nancy Cantor, 15-31. New York: Springer-Verlag, 1989.

———. "Personal Project Pursuit: Dimensions and Dynamics of Personal Meaning." In *Human Quest for Meaning: A Handbook of Psychological Research and Clinical Applications*, edited by Paul T. P. Wong and Prem S. Fry, 197-221. Mahwah, NJ: Lawrence Erlbaum Associates, 1998.

———. "Personal Projects and Social Ecology: Themes and Variations Across the Life Span." In *Action and Self-Development: Theory and Research Through the Life Span*, edited by Jochen Brandtstädter and Richard M. Lerner, 197-221. Thousand Oaks, CA: Sage, 1999.

———. "Personality and Motivation: Personal Action and the Conative Evolution." In *Handbook of Personality: Theory and Research* (2nd ed.), edited by Lawrence A. Pervin and Oliver P. John, 501-524. New York: Guilford Press, 1999.

———. "Free Traits and Personal Contexts: Expanding a Social Ecological Model of Well-Being." In *Person-Environment Psychology: New Directions and Perspectives* (2nd ed.), edited by W. Bruce Walsh, Kenneth H. Craik, and Richard H. Price, 87–116. Mahwah, NJ: Lawrence Erlbaum Associates, 2000.

———. "Personality Science and Self-Regulation: Personal Projects as Integrative Units." *Applied Psychology: An International Review* 55, no. 3 (2006): 419–427.

———. "Prompt and Circumstance: The Generative Contexts of Personal Projects Analysis." In *Personal Project Pursuit: Goals, Action, and Human Flourishing*, edited by Brian R. Little, Katariina Salmela-Aro, and Susan D. Phillips, 3–49. Mahwah, NJ: Lawrence Erlbaum Associates, 2007.

———. "Opening Space for Project Pursuit: Affordance, Restoration and Chills." In *Innovative Approaches to Researching Landscape and Health. Open Space: People Space 2*, edited by Catharine Ward Thompson, Peter Aspinall, and Simon Bell, 163–178. New York: Routledge, 2010.

———. "Personality Science and the Northern Tilt: As Positive as Possible Under the Circumstances." In *Designing Positive Psychology: Taking Stock and Moving Forward*, edited by Kennon M. Sheldon, Todd B. Kashdan, and Michael F. Steger, 228–247. New York: Oxford University Press, 2011.

———. *Me, Myself and Us: The Science of Personality and the Art of Well-Being*. New York: PublicAffairs, 2014.

———. "Well-Doing: Personal Projects and the Quality of Lives." *Theory and Research in Education* 12 (2014): 329–346.

Little, Brian R., and David M. Frost. "Aspects of Love: Connecting, Romancing, and Caring." In *Positive Psychology of Love*, edited by M. Hojjat and Duncan Cramer, 162–176. New York: Oxford University Press, 2013.

Little, Brian R., and Maryann F. Joseph. "Personal Projects and Free Traits: Mutable Selves and Well-Beings." In *Personal Project Pursuit: Goals, Action, and Human Flourishing*, edited by Brian R. Little, Katariina Salmela-Aro, and Susan D. Phillips, 375–400. Mahwah, NJ: Lawrence Erlbaum Associates, 2007.

Little, Brian R., Len Lecci, and Barbara Watkinson. "Personality and Personal Projects: Linking Big Five and PAC Units of Analysis." *Journal of Personality* 60, no. 2 (1992): 501–525.

Little, Brian R., Katariina Salmela-Aro, and Susan D. Phillips, eds. *Personal Project Pursuit: Goals, Action, and Human Flourishing*. Mahwah, NJ: Lawrence Erlbaum Associates, 2007.

Lomasky, Loren E. "Personal Projects as the Foundation for Basic Rights." *Social Philosophy and Policy* 1, no. 2 (1984): 35–55.

MacKinnon, Donald W. "The Nature and Nurture of Creative Talent." *American Psychologist* 17, no. 7 (1962): 484–495. doi:10.1037/h0046541.

McCrae, Robert R. "Aesthetic Chills as a Universal Marker of Openness to Experience." *Motivation and Emotion* 31, no. 1 (2007): 5–11.

Nettle, Daniel. *Personality: What Makes You the Way You Are*. New York: Oxford University Press, 2007.

Ozer, Daniel J., and Verónica Benet-Martínez. "Personality and the Prediction of Consequential Outcomes." *Annual Review of Psychology* 57 (2006): 401–421.

Palys, Ted S., and Brian R. Little. "Perceived Life Satisfaction and the Organization of Personal Project Systems." *Journal of Personality and Social Psychology* 44, no. 6 (1983): 1221–1230.

Phillips, Susan D., Brian R. Little, and Laura A. Goodine, "Reconsidering Gender and Public Administration: Five Steps Beyond Conventional Research." *Canadian Public Administration* 40, no. 4 (1997): 563–581.

Roberts, Brent W., Kate E. Walton, and Tim Bogg. "Conscientiousness and Health Across the Life Course." *Review of General Psychology* 9, no. 2 (2005): 156–168.

Rosenzweig, Mark R., David Krech, Edward L. Bennett, and Marian C. Diamond. "Effects of Environmental Complexity and Training on Brain Chemistry and Anatomy: A Replication and Extension." *Journal of Comparative and Physiological Psychology* 55 (1962): 429–437.

Ruehlman, Linda S., and Sharlene A. Wolchik. "Personal Goals and Interpersonal Support and Hindrance as Factors in Psychological Distress and Well-Being." *Journal of Personality and Social Psychology* 55 (1988): 293–301.

Salmela-Aro, Katariina. "Struggling with Self: The Personal Projects of Students Seeking Psychological Counselling." *Scandinavian Journal of Psychology* 33, no. 4 (1992): 330–338.

Seligman, Martin E. P., Peter Railton, Roy F. Baumeister, and Chandra Sripada. *Homo Prospectus*. New York: Oxford University Press, 2016.

Serraino, Pierluigi. *The Creative Architect: Inside the Great Midcentury Personality Study*. New York: Monacelli Press, 2016.

Snyder, Mark. *Public Appearances, Private Realities: The Psychology of Self-Monitoring*. New York: W. H. Freeman, 1987.

Thacker, Karissa. *The Art of Authenticity: Tools to Become an Authentic Leader and Your Best Self*. New York: Wiley, 2016.

Tiberius, Valerie. *The Reflective Life: Living Wisely with Our Limits*. New York: Oxford University Press, 2008.

Williams, Bernard. *Moral Luck*. Cambridge, UK: Cambridge University Press, 1982.

Wilt, Joshua, and William Revelle. "Extraversion." In *Handbook of Individual Differences in Social Behavior*, edited by Mark R. Leary and Rick H. Hoyle, 27–45. New York: Guilford Press, 2009.

Dr. Brian R. Little is an internationally acclaimed scholar and speaker in the field of personality and motivational psychology. His pioneering research on how everyday personal projects and "free traits" influence the course of our lives has become an important way of explaining and enhancing human flourishing. Professor Little is currently at Cambridge University where he is a fellow of the Well-being Institute and director of the Social Ecology Research Group in the Department of Psychology. He is also affiliated with the Cambridge Judge Business School and the Psychometrics Centre at Cambridge.

Previously, he taught at McGill, Oxford, and Harvard Universities. His course on personality in Harvard's Department of Psychology was immensely popular, and he was elected as a "Favorite Professor" by the graduating classes of Harvard for three consecutive years. Dividing his time between Canada and the UK, Brian is also a distinguished research professor emeritus at Carleton University in Ottawa and he lectures worldwide on personality, motivation, and well-being.

WATCH BRIAN R. LITTLE'S TED TALK

Brian R. Little's TED Talk, available for free at
TED.com, is the companion to *Who Are You, Really?*

PHOTO: BRET HARTMAN/TED

Dan Gilbert
The Psychology of Your Future Self
"Human beings are works in progress that mistakenly think they're finished." Dan Gilbert shares recent research on a phenomenon he calls the "end of history illusion," where we somehow imagine that the person we are right now is the person we'll be for the rest of time. Hint: that's not the case.

Susan Cain
The Power of Introverts
In a culture where being social and outgoing are prized above all else, it can be difficult, even shameful, to be an introvert. But, as Susan Cain argues in this passionate talk, introverts bring extraordinary talents and abilities to the world, and should be encouraged and celebrated.

Julian Baggini
Is There a Real You?
What makes you, you? Is it how you think of yourself, how others think of you, or something else entirely? Philosopher Julian Baggini draws from philosophy and neuroscience to give a surprising answer.

Dan Ariely
Are We in Control of Our Own Decisions?
Behavioral economist Dan Ariely, the author of *Predictably Irrational*, uses classic visual illusions and his own counterintuitive (and sometimes shocking) research findings to show how we're not as rational as we think when we make decisions.

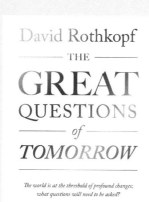

The Great Questions of Tomorrow
by David Rothkopf

We are on the cusp of a sweeping revolution—one that will change every facet of our lives. The changes ahead will challenge and alter fundamental concepts such as national identity, human rights, money and markets. In this pivotal, complicated moment, what are the great questions we need to ask to navigate our way forward?

Payoff: The Hidden Logic That Shapes Our Motivation
by Dan Ariely

Payoff investigates the true nature of motivation, our partial blindness to the way it works, and how we can bridge this gap. Dan Ariely digs deep to find the root of motivation—how it works and how we can use this knowledge to approach important choices in our own lives.

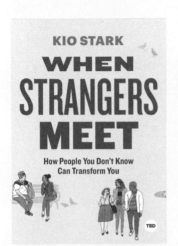

When Strangers Meet: How People You Don't Know Can Transform You
by Kio Stark

When Strangers Meet reveals the transformative possibility of talking to people you don't know—how these beautiful interruptions in daily life can change you and the world we share. Kio Stark argues for the surprising pleasures of talking to strangers.

Asteroid Hunters
by Carrie Nugent

Everyone's got questions about asteroids. What are they and where do they come from? And most urgently: Are they going to hit Earth? Asteroid hunter Carrie Nugent reveals everything we know about asteroids, and how new technology may help us prevent a natural disaster.

TED is a nonprofit devoted to spreading ideas, usually in the form of short, powerful talks (eighteen minutes or less) but also through books, animation, radio programs, and events. TED began in 1984 as a conference where Technology, Entertainment, and Design converged, and today covers almost every topic— from science to business to global issues—in more than one hundred languages. Meanwhile, independently run TEDx events help share ideas in communities around the world.

TED is a global community, welcoming people from every discipline and culture who seek a deeper understanding of the world. We believe passionately in the power of ideas to change attitudes, lives, and, ultimately, our future. On TED.com, we're building a clearinghouse of free knowledge from the world's most inspired thinkers—and a community of curious souls to engage with ideas and each other, both online and at TED and TEDx events around the world, all year long.

In fact, everything we do—from the TED Radio Hour to the projects sparked by the TED Prize, from the global TEDx community to the TED-Ed lesson series — is driven by this goal: How can we best spread great ideas?

TED is owned by a nonprofit, nonpartisan foundation.